THE

CAKE LOOKS GREAT

Dialogs & Stories

WILLIAM P. PICKETT
Passaic High School

PEARSON
Longman

The Cake Looks Great: Dialogs & Stories

Pearson Education, 10 Bank Street, White Plains, NY 10606

Staff credits: The people who made up *The Cake Looks Great: Dialogs & Stories* team,
representing editorial, production, design, and manufacturing, are Pietro Alongi,
Christine Edmonds, Nancy Flaggman, Malgorzata Jaros-White, Laura Le Dréan,
Jaime E. Lieber, Michael Mone, Liza Pleva, and Patricia Wosczyk.
Cover design: Patricia Wosczyk
Text composition: Integra
Text font: 11.5/12.5pt ITC Century Book

ISBN-10: 0-13-233093-8
ISBN-13: 978-0-13-233093-0

Library of Congress Cataloging-in-Publication Data

Pickett, William P., 1931–
    The cake looks great: dialogs & stories/William P. Pickett.
        p. cm.
    ISBN 0-13-233093-8 (pbk.)
    1. English language—Textbooks for foreign speakers.   2. Readers (Adult)   I. Title.
PE1128P469 2008
428.6'4—dc22

                                                                    2007039838

Printed in the United States of America
2 3 4 5 6 7 8 9 10–V0N4–11 10

To Ed and Colleen

Contents

4 Jobs 67

5 Exercise and Sports 89

6 Learning 111

Preface

OVERVIEW

The Cake Looks Great is a low-beginning reader featuring thirty-two dialogs and eight two-part stories. The dialogs and stories are about people and everyday happenings that students can easily identify with. The book is about the joys and struggles, the hopes and fears, the light moments and the serious ones of ordinary people.

Above all, *The Cake* aims to be interesting and easy, a book that students will enjoy as they take their first steps in reading. Its style is colloquial, and its vocabulary and grammar are informal. It includes a variety of themes, settings, and characters.

Many of the dialogs and stories are about newcomers to the United States. In them, you will meet people from Peru, Poland, Mexico, Italy, the Dominican Republic, Haiti, India, and China.

LEVEL

Like *The Pizza Tastes Great*, *The Cake Looks Great* is written for beginners. However, the dialogs and stories of *The Cake* are shorter and written for a lower level than *The Pizza*. Easy-to-understand vocabulary and structures are used. Students who are just beginning to learn English can use *The Cake*.

OBJECTIVES

The Cake Looks Great aims to
1. provide interesting and easy reading material to improve reading skills,
2. expand vocabulary,
3. improve listening comprehension, and
4. increase fluency through discussion.

AUDIENCE

The Cake is written for adults of all ages. It can be used successfully in middle schools, high schools, two-year colleges, adult education classes, and for home study. It can even be used in those four-year colleges that accept students who don't know any English.

CONTENTS

A. Word Banks

All the dialogs and stories in *The Cake Looks Great* are preceded by a Word Bank to help the students understand the key words in the dialog or story. The entries in the Word Bank are followed by an example sentence. Especially at the beginning level, an example sentence is likely to be more helpful than a definition. The example sentences are in italics and the key words are underlined.

A definition or explanation of the key word comes after the example sentence. Most words are defined. Words that cannot be defined in a way that will help beginners are explained.

Since the Word Bank is a glossary, it generally includes only the meaning each word has in the dialog or story. Sometimes this is not the most common meaning of the word. In these cases, the teacher may wish to mention the more common meaning.

Although the Word Bank is placed before the dialog or story, some teachers and students may prefer to use the Word Bank *after* reading the dialog or story. Teachers are encouraged to experiment to see which order best suits their teaching style and the learning styles of their students.

In any case, *The Cake* is a reader to be enjoyed, not a vocabulary book to be studied, so too much time should not be spent on the Word Bank.

B. Preview Questions

All the dialogs and stories are introduced by two preview questions to help the students recall what they already know about the subject and to stimulate their interest in it.

C. Dialogs and Stories

The dialogs and stories are the heart of *The Cake*. Everything in the book either leads up to or flows from them. If a student reads, understands, and enjoys them, he or she will become a better reader. Most teachers read the dialogs and stories aloud to their students while the students listen to and read them to themselves.

Every chapter of *The Cake* contains four dialogs and a two-part story. The dialogs are ten lines long and are meant to be used for role-playing as well as reading. The stories are divided into two parts, and each part has three to five paragraphs.

D. Comprehension Questions

Comprehension questions immediately follow all the dialogs and stories. Most of the questions are factual, but one of them has an asterisk

and requires the students to think beyond the text and make inferences or give their opinions.

E. Sharing Information

The sharing-information section follows the comprehension questions. This section encourages students to discuss topics related to the dialogs and stories. It gives them the opportunity to talk about their own ideas, feelings, and lives. This will be difficult for most students at this level, and some of them may only be able to listen to the other students and say a few words.

F. Sentence-Completion Exercises

Sentence-completion exercises test and reinforce the vocabulary used in the dialogs and stories. Increasing students' vocabulary is one of the major aims of *The Cake*, and the sentence-completion exercises help solidify and enlarge the reader's vocabulary.

G. Matching Exercises

On the last page of each chapter there are two matching exercises. The first one reviews words from the dialogs. The second reviews words from the stories.

I. Word List

In the back of this book, there is an alphabetical list of all the words defined or explained in the Word Banks.

REVIEW TESTS, ANSWER KEY, AND AUDIO CDs

A separate booklet contains eight vocabulary tests, one for each chapter. The booklet also has an Answer Key with the answers to the exercises in *The Cake* and to the vocabulary tests in the booklet. Audio CDs with all the dialogs and stories are also available.

FOUR-LEVEL SERIES

The Cake Looks Great, The Pizza Tastes Great, The Salsa Is Hot, and *The Chicken Smells Good* form a series. *The Cake* and *The Pizza* are written for beginners. However, the dialogs and stories of *The Cake* are shorter and easier. The Salsa is written for advanced beginners, and *The Chicken* for low intermediate students.

The hallmark of this series is its combination of interesting dialogs and stories about people the students can identify with. Students enjoy reading and discussing these dialogs and stories, and learn a lot of English while doing so.

ACKNOWLEDGMENTS

I am very grateful to Laura Le Dréan, my acquisitions editor, for her assistance in writing *The Cake Looks Great*. Her suggestions and enthusiasm were most helpful. I also wish to thank Gosia Jaros-White, my development editor, and Michael Mone, my production editor, for their excellent work. Both were very helpful.

The artwork of Don Martinetti captures the spirit of the dialogs and stories and illustrates them well. He has added a great deal to *The Cake*, and I am grateful to him.

Above all, I wish to thank my wife, Dorothy, who went over every story and dialog with great care and made many valuable suggestions. Finally, I am grateful to my son, Ed, whose comments and suggestions helped me rewrite parts of *The Cake*.

1 Newcomers to the United States

Here are the people you will meet in the dialogs and stories in this chapter.

Maria   Roberto   Manny   Rosa

Henry   Jan   Anna

José   Blanca   Ramón   Carmen

Glad to Meet You

WORD BANK

1. **hello, hi**   *"Hello, Pete." "Hi, Tom. How are you?"* **Hi** is a short form of **hello**.
2. **where**   *Where do you live?* **Where** means in what place.
3. **Poland**   *Poland is between Russia and Germany.* **Poland** is a country in Europe.
4. **Peru**   *Peru is on the Pacific Ocean.* **Peru** is a country in South America.
5. **meet**   *I want you to meet my friend Sara.* To **meet** is to see and say hello to a person for the first time.
6. **happy**   *I'm happy you're in my class.* **Happy** means feeling very good.
7. **glad**   *We're glad you like your job.* **Glad** means feeling very good.

PREVIEW QUESTIONS

Discuss these questions before listening to and reading the dialog.

1. What is your name?
2. What country are you from?

Henry and Maria go to school at night to learn English. They're in the same class. They meet after class.

Henry: Hello, my name is Henry.
Maria: Hi, my name is Maria.
Henry: Where are you from?
Maria: Peru. And you?
Henry: Poland.
Maria: Happy to meet you!
Henry: Glad to meet you!

COMPREHENSION

Answer these questions about the dialog. Use your own ideas to answer the question with an asterisk. (is an asterisk.)*

1. What does Maria say to Henry?
2. Where is Maria from?
3. Where is Henry from?
4. How does Maria feel about meeting Henry?
5. How does he feel about meeting her?
*6. Do you like to meet new people?

SHARING INFORMATION

Discuss these questions in pairs, in small groups, or with the whole class.

1. What language do you speak?
2. How long have you been in the United States?

SENTENCE COMPLETION

Complete the sentences with these words.

hi	where	happy

1. _____ are you going?
2. _____, Sam. It's good to see you.
3. I'm _____ you're coming to our party.

from	meet	glad

4. I'm _____ it's a nice day.
5. Shanta lives in the United States, but she's _____ India.
6. Erik wants us to _____ his friend.

DIALOG REVIEW

Two students come to the front of the class and use this dialog to meet. The other students listen. Then the other students use the dialog to meet. After meeting, the students shake hands.

Glad to Meet You

A: Hello, my name is _____.

B: Hi, my name is _____.

A: Where are you from?

B: _____. And you?

A: _____.

B: Happy to meet you!

A: Glad to meet you!

A Birthday Party

WORD BANK

1. **Manny's**   *Maria is <u>Manny's</u> mother.* **Manny's** = of Manny
2. **how**   *<u>How</u> big is your class?* **How** begins a question.
3. **he's**   *<u>He's</u> a student.* **he's** = he is
4. **who's**   *<u>Who's</u> playing with our son?* **who's** = who is
5. **friend**   *Vicky likes Lisa, and they play after school. They're <u>friends</u>.* A **friend** is a person that you know and like very much.
6. **very**   *In January, it's <u>very</u> cold in Canada.* A person who is 87 is old. A person who is 97 is **very** old.
7. **that's**   *<u>That's</u> a nice car.* **that's** = that is

PREVIEW QUESTIONS

Discuss these questions before listening to and reading the dialog.

1. Why do children like birthdays?
2. Who comes to a child's birthday?

Maria is talking to Henry before class. Today is her son's birthday. His name is Manny.

Maria: Today is Manny's birthday.

Henry: How old is he?

Maria: He's nine.

Henry: Is he having a party?

Maria: Yes, he is.

Henry: Who's coming to the party?

Maria: All of his friends.

Henry: That's good.

Maria: Yes. He's very happy.

COMPREHENSION

If the sentence is true, write T. *If it's false, write* F.

____T____ 1. Today is Manny's birthday.
_____ 2. He's 10 years old.
_____ 3. He's having a party.
_____ 4. All his friends are coming to the party.
_____ 5. He's not happy.

SHARING INFORMATION

Discuss these questions in pairs, in small groups, or with the whole class.

1. When is your birthday?
2. Do you do anything special on your birthday?

SENTENCE COMPLETION

Complete the sentences with these words.

birthday	how	good	who's

1. _____ cold is it? Do I need a hat?
2. _____ in the kitchen?
3. May 9 is my _____. When is your birthday?
4. This cake is _____.

come	all	friends	very

5. I like Beth and she likes me. We're _____.
6. _____ here. I want to give you something.
7. In July, it's _____ hot in Florida.
8. _____ of the students are reading.

MAKING COMPLETE SENTENCES

Draw lines from column A to column B to make complete sentences.

A	B
1. Everyone is wishing Mario	is your son?
2. How tall	35 years old today.
3. I'm happy	to Linda?
4. Who's talking	a happy birthday.
5. Mario is	to see you.

Make complete sentences by joining the words from columns A and B.

Example

1. *Everyone is wishing Mario a happy birthday.* _____
2. _____
3. _____
4. _____
5. _____

Dinner Is Ready

WORD BANK

1. **newspaper**   *Larry reads the <u>newspaper</u> every morning.* A **newspaper** is a printed report on what is happening in the world.
2. **dinner**   *We always eat <u>dinner</u> at six o'clock.* **Dinner** is the big meal of the day.
3. **ready**   *The children are <u>ready</u> to go to school.* **Ready** means prepared to.
4. **hungry**   *I'm <u>hungry</u>. When are we going to eat?* **Hungry** means wanting to eat.
5. **homework**   *Most students don't like <u>homework</u>, but it helps them to learn.* **Homework** is school work a student does at home.
6. **cell phone**   *Jamie always takes her <u>cell phone</u> to work.* A **cell phone** is a small phone you can carry with you.
7. **too**   *I think Pat talks <u>too</u> much.* **Too** means more than is good.

PREVIEW QUESTIONS

Discuss these questions before listening to and reading the dialog.

1. Do you read a newspaper? How often do you read a newspaper?
2. What time do you eat dinner?

Maria and her son, Manny, are in the kitchen. Dinner is ready. Maria wants her husband, Roberto, and her daughter, Rosa, to come to dinner. Rosa is 16.

Maria:	Roberto! What are you doing?
Roberto:	Reading the newspaper.
Maria:	Dinner is ready.
Roberto:	Good, I'm hungry.
Maria:	Where's Rosa?
Roberto:	In her room.
Maria:	Is she doing her homework?
Roberto:	No, she's talking on her cell phone.
Maria:	She's on the phone too much.
Roberto:	I know.

COMPREHENSION

Answer these questions about the dialog. Use your own ideas to answer the question with an asterisk.

1. What is Roberto doing?
2. What does Maria tell Roberto?
3. Where's Rosa?
4. What's she doing?
5. How much is she on the cell phone?
*6. Who do you think she's talking to?

SHARING INFORMATION

Discuss these questions in pairs, in small groups, or with the whole class.

1. Do you have a cell phone?
2. How much do you use a cell phone?

SENTENCE COMPLETION

Complete the sentences with these words.

newspaper	too	cell phone	dinner

1. It's _____ cold to go swimming.
2. What are we having to eat for _____?
3. Ed reads the _____ when he comes home from work.
4. Can I use your _____ to make a call?

reading	hungry	homework	ready

5. Is everything _____ for the party?
6. Terry is _____ a book.
7. The students are happy. They don't have any _____.
8. It's three o'clock and we didn't eat lunch. We're _____.

DIALOG REVIEW

Complete the paragraphs with these words.

It's Time to Eat

ready	hungry	newspaper	dinner

Roberto is reading the _____. Maria tells him that _____ is _____. Roberto says that's good. He's _____.

cell phone	homework	too	room

Rosa is in her _____. She isn't doing her _____. She's talking on her _____. She talks on it _____ much.

A Math Test

WORD BANK

1. **tired**   *I did a lot of work today. I'm <u>tired</u>.* A person who is **tired** needs rest or sleep.
2. **can't**   *Phil <u>can't</u> go to the party. He's sick.* **Can't** means not able to.
3. **test**   *There are 20 questions on the science <u>test</u>.* A **test** is a group of questions used to see how much a student knows.
4. **tomorrow**   *Today is Sunday. <u>Tomorrow</u> is Monday.* **Tomorrow** is the day after today.
5. **subject**   *Math, English, history, and science are <u>subjects</u>.* **Subjects** are what you study in school.
6. **hard**   *The president of the United States has a <u>hard</u> job.* **Hard** means not easy; difficult.

PREVIEW QUESTIONS

Discuss these questions before reading and listening to the dialog.

1. Do you think math is an important subject?
2. Do you like math?

Henry has two children, Anna and Jan. They're high school students. Jan is studying for a math test. It's 10:00 P.M. He is talking to Anna.

Jan:	I'm tired.
Anna:	Go to bed.
Jan:	I can't.
Anna:	Why not?
Jan:	I'm studying. I have a test tomorrow.
Anna:	In what subject?
Jan:	Math.
Anna:	Who's your teacher?
Jan:	Mr. Patel.
Anna:	Oh no! He gives hard tests.

COMPREHENSION

Answer these questions about the dialog. Use your own ideas to answer the question with an asterisk.

1. How does Jan feel?
2. Why can't he go to bed?
3. In what subject does he have a test?
4. Who's his teacher?
5. Are Mr. Patel's tests easy or hard?
*6. Do you think math is a hard subject? Explain your answer.

SHARING INFORMATION

Discuss these questions in pairs, in small groups, or with the whole class.

1. What is your favorite subject?
2. What is the problem with going to bed late the night before a test?

SENTENCE COMPLETION

Complete the sentences with these words.

tired	beds	can't	test

1. How many _____ are in the room?
2. I got 100 on my history _____. It was easy.
3. Carlos _____ speak English.
4. I'm going to sit down and rest. I'm _____.

tomorrow	subjects	who's	hard

5. _____ at the door?
6. The bank is closed. I'll go to the bank _____.
7. It's _____ to learn English.
8. Elena is a good student and likes all her _____.

MAKING COMPLETE SENTENCES

Draw lines from column A to column B to make complete sentences.

A	**B**
1. When Kevin gets home from work,	at school tomorrow.
2. I will see you	get up in the morning.
3. What subject does	like to go to bed.
4. Sometimes it's hard to	he's tired.
5. Many children don't	Mrs. Hogan teach?

Make complete sentences by joining the words from columns A and B.

Example

1. *When Kevin gets home from work, he's tired.* _____
2. _____
3. _____
4. _____
5. _____

From Mexico to the United States

WORD BANK

1. **live**   *Frank lives and works in Boston.* To **live** is to have a home in.
2. **married**   *Caroline is married. I know her husband.* **Married** means having a husband or wife.
3. **wife**   *Leslie and I are married. She's my wife and I'm her husband.* A **wife** is a married woman. A husband is a married man.
4. **also**   *Pedro speaks Spanish. Pablo also speaks Spanish.* **Also** means *too.*
5. **child**   (plural – **children**) *I have one child. My friend has two children, a boy and a girl.* A **child** is a son or daughter; any young boy or girl.
6. **apartment**   *I'm looking for a large apartment in a nice building.* An **apartment** is a group of rooms that people live in.
7. **bedroom**   *Our house has three bedrooms.* A **bedroom** is a room for sleeping and has one or more beds.
8. **living room**   *George is in the living room talking to his brother.* A **living room** is a room where we sit to talk, read, and watch TV.
9. **pay**   *How much did you pay for the coat?* To **pay** is to give someone money for something.
10. **rent**   *I pay the rent on the first day of the month.* **Rent** is the money that you pay to use an apartment, home, or office.

PREVIEW QUESTIONS

Discuss these questions before listening to and reading the story.

1. In what city do you live?
2. In what state do you live?

José Garcia lives in San Diego, California. He's from Puebla, Mexico. He's 40 years old.

José is married. His wife is also from Puebla. Her name is Blanca. She's 35 years old. José and Blanca have two children, Ramón and Carmen. Ramón is 15. Carmen is 12.

José and Blanca live in an apartment on Brook Avenue. It's a nice apartment. It has two small bedrooms and one large one. The living room is also large. José and Blanca pay a thousand dollars a month in rent. They like their apartment.

COMPREHENSION

Answer these questions about the story. Use your own ideas to answer the question with an asterisk.

Paragraph 1

1. Where does José live?
2. Where is he from?
3. How old is he?

Paragraph 2

4. How old is Blanca?
5. How many children do José and Blanca have?
6. What are their names?

Paragraph 3

7. What avenue do José and Blanca live on?
8. How many bedrooms does their apartment have?
9. How much rent do they pay?
*10. Why do you think that José and Blanca like their apartment?

SHARING INFORMATION

Discuss these questions in pairs, in small groups, or with the whole class.

1. Do you live in an apartment or a house?
2. How big is your apartment or house?
3. Are you happy with your apartment or house? Explain your answer.
4. How is your apartment or house in the United States different from where you lived in your home country?

SENTENCE COMPLETION

Complete the sentences with these words.

large	bedroom	lives	also

1. My brother _____ in Texas.
2. Texas is a _____ state.
3. I am a nurse. My daughter is _____ a nurse.
4. You can use the telephone in my _____.

apartment	children	small	pay

5. The _____ are watching TV.
6. Let me _____ for your lunch.
7. Our house is _____, but we like it.
8. How many rooms does your _____ have?

wife	married	living room	rent

9. Are you single or _____?
10. How much is the _____ for this apartment?
11. Don and his _____ are going to the movies.
12. Sue is reading a book in the _____.

A Family at Work and at School

1. **restaurant**   *I know a <u>restaurant</u> that has very good food.* A **restaurant** is a place where you go to eat.
2. **job**   *Reggie is a police officer and he likes his <u>job</u>.* A **job** is work that you do to make money.
3. **well**   *Brian plays the piano <u>well</u>.* **Well** means in a good way.
4. **teacher's assistant**   *Pamela is working with a small group of students in the back of the class. She's a <u>teacher's assistant</u>.* A **teacher's assistant** helps a teacher do his or her job.
5. **grade**   *My daughter is in the second <u>grade</u>. My son is in the seventh <u>grade</u>.* A **grade** is a class level.
6. **young**   *Paul is 20. He's a <u>young</u> man.* **Young** means not old.
7. **favorite**   *I love basketball. It's my <u>favorite</u> sport.* **Favorite** means liked the most.
8. **soccer**   *Our school has a very good <u>soccer</u> team this year.* **Soccer** is a game in which you move the ball by kicking it.
9. **volleyball**   *Amy is a good <u>volleyball</u> player. She's tall and hits the ball hard.* **Volleyball** is a game in which the players try to keep the ball from hitting the ground.

PREVIEW QUESTIONS

Discuss these questions before listening to and reading the story.

1. Do you think that most people in the United States work hard?
2. Do you think that most newcomers to the United States also work hard?

José and his wife, Blanca, are doing well in the United States. Their two children, Carmen and Ramón, are also doing well.

José is a cook at a Mexican restaurant in San Diego. His job isn't easy. He works six days a week, 10 hours a day. José likes to cook. He's a good cook.

Blanca works at Number 3 School. She's a teacher's assistant. She helps the first-grade teacher. It's a good job for Blanca. She loves working with young children. Her pay is good.

Carmen goes to Lincoln Middle School. She's in the seventh grade. She's a very good student. Her favorite subject is math. She also likes to play volleyball.

Ramón goes to Kennedy High School. He's in the 10th grade. He doesn't like to study, but he does well in all of his subjects. He says that lunch is his favorite subject. He's a very good soccer player.

COMPREHENSION

Answer these questions about the story. Use your own ideas to answer the question with an asterisk.

Paragraph 1

1. How are José, Blanca, and their two children doing in the United States?

Paragraph 2

2. What is José's job?
3. Is his job easy or hard?
4. How many hours a week does he work?

Paragraph 3

5. What is Blanca's job?
6. Who does she help?
7. Why is this a good job for Blanca? Give two reasons.

Paragraph 4

8. What grade is Carmen in?
9. What's her favorite subject?
10. What sport does she like to play?

Paragraph 5

11. What grade is Ramón in?
12. What does he say is his favorite subject?
13. What sport does he play?
*14. Do you think he likes school? Explain your answer.

SHARING INFORMATION

Discuss these questions in pairs, in small groups, or with the whole class.

1. Do you think José cooks much at home? Explain your answer.
2. Would you like to be a teacher or a teacher's assistant? Explain your answer.
3. Why is a teacher's job important?
4. What was or is your hardest subject?

SENTENCE COMPLETION

Complete the sentences with these words.

well	cooks	job	restaurants

1. A student's _____ is to study and learn.
2. My wife and I aren't good _____.
3. That's why we love to eat in _____.
4. Kristin is a good driver. She drives _____.

grade	easy	young	soccer

5. When you play _____, you run a lot and get tired.
6. It's not _____ to be a teacher.
7. Jimmy is 11. He's in the sixth _____.
8. I think Jimmy is too _____ to work after school.

hours	favorite	teacher's assistant	volleyball

9. The _____ is helping the students with their math.
10. You can drive from New York City to Washington, D.C., in four
    _____.
11. The students are playing _____ in the schoolyard.
12. What is your _____ TV program?

MATCHING

Match the words in Column A with their definitions or descriptions in Column B. Print the letters on the blank lines.

Words from the Dialogs

	Column A	Column B
_____	**1.** glad	**A.** the big meal of the day
_____	**2.** tomorrow	**B.** needing rest
_____	**3.** hungry	**C.** prepared to act
_____	**4.** dinner	**D.** the day after today
_____	**5.** ready	**E.** difficult
_____	**6.** hard	**F.** happy
_____	**7.** tired	**G.** in what place
_____	**8.** where	**H.** wanting to eat

Words from the Stories

	Column A	Column B
_____	**1.** job	**A.** liked the most
_____	**2.** restaurant	**B.** a married woman
_____	**3.** wife	**C.** not old
_____	**4.** living room	**D.** money you pay to use something
_____	**5.** young	**E.** a place to eat
_____	**6.** favorite	**F.** a boy or girl
_____	**7.** rent	**G.** work you do for money
_____	**8.** child	**H.** a room to sit, talk, or watch TV

2 Love

Here are the people you will meet in the dialogs and stories in this chapter.

Mike

Kristin

Tom

Grandma

Debra

Mrs. Flores

Jackie

Pete

A Nice Girl

WORD BANK

1. **sorry** *I'm sorry your mother is in the hospital.* To be **sorry** is to feel bad (unhappy) about something.

2. **problem** *I'm having a lot of problems with my car. I'm going to buy a new one.* A **problem** is a difficult situation that you must do something about.

3. **boyfriend** *Ted is my boyfriend. We go to the movies and out to dinner a lot.* A **boyfriend** is a boy or man who is your friend, and the friendship is romantic.

4. **invite** *Kathy is inviting me to her party.* To **invite** is to ask a person to come to something, for example, a party or dinner.

PREVIEW QUESTIONS

Discuss these questions before listening to and reading the dialog.

1. Do you like to go to the movies?
2. How often do you go?

Mike meets Kristin at a party. He likes Kristin and thinks she's very nice. He wants to take her to a movie.

Mike:	You're very nice.
Kristin:	Thank you.
Mike:	Do you like to go to movies?
Kristin:	Yes, I do.
Mike:	Can I take you to a movie?
Kristin:	I can't go with you. I'm sorry.
Mike:	What's the problem?
Kristin:	I have a boyfriend.
Mike:	I understand.
Kristin:	Thanks for inviting me.

COMPREHENSION

Answer these questions about the dialog. Use your own ideas to answer the question with an asterisk.

1. What does Kristin say when Mike tells her she's nice?
2. Does she like to go to movies?
3. Is she going to go to a movie with Mike?
4. Why can't she go with him?
5. What does he say when Kristin tells him she has a boyfriend?
*6. Do you think she likes Mike? Explain your answer.

SHARING INFORMATION

Discuss these questions in pairs, in small groups, or with the whole class.

1. Do you ever rent movies to watch at home? How often?
2. Which do you like more? To go out to a movie or to rent a movie to watch at home?

SENTENCE COMPLETION

Complete the sentences with these words.

problem	can't	nice	sorry

1. The baby _____ walk. She's only 10 months old.
2. I'm _____ I'm late.
3. We like Joe. He's very _____.
4. Rita doesn't have a job. It's a big _____.

invite	very	understand	boyfriend

5. Fred can't come to our party, but I _____. He has to work the night of the party.
6. We're going to _____ Yoko to our house for dinner.
7. Brenda likes Doug a lot, but he isn't her _____.
8. Scott's computer is _____ old. He needs a new one.

MAKING COMPLETE SENTENCES

Draw lines from column A to column B to make complete sentences.

A	B
1. Did Tony invite you	and I'll help you.
2. Marissa is nice	go to the game with you.
3. I understand your problem	and also pretty.
4. Our math teacher	to the picnic?
5. I'm sorry I can't	is very young.

Make complete sentences by joining the words from columns A and B.

Example

1. *Did Tony invite you to the picnic?* _____
2. _____
3. _____
4. _____
5. _____

Very Happy

1. **look**   *Dan works a lot. He _looks_ tired.* To **look** is to appear to be.
2. **lucky**   *Adrian was in a bad accident, but he's OK. He's _lucky_.* **Lucky** means having good luck. Luck is what happens to you by chance.
3. **how**   *_How_ do you go to work? _How_ do you know Monica is rich?* **How** means in what way. How asks in what way you do or know something.
4. **marry**   *Jason is going to _marry_ Lisa in June.* To **marry** is to become someone's husband or wife.

PREVIEW QUESTIONS

Discuss these questions before listening to and reading the dialog.

1. Does love make people happy?
2. Name a person that you love a lot.

Victor is talking to his cousin Kristin. Kristin is the one Mike wanted to take to the movies. She's in love with Tom Martin. She wants to marry him. Kristin is 21; Tom is 23.

Victor:	You look very happy.
Kristin:	I am.
Victor:	Why?
Kristin:	I'm in love.
Victor:	Who's the lucky young man?
Kristin:	Tom Martin.
Victor:	How do you know you love him?
Kristin:	I think about him all the time.
Victor:	Do you want to marry him?
Kristin:	Yes, I do.

COMPREHENSION

If the sentence is true, write T. *If it's false, write* F.

_____ 1. Kristin is unhappy.
_____ 2. She's in love.
_____ 3. Victor thinks Tom is lucky.
_____ 4. Kristin doesn't think about Tom much.
_____ 5. She wants to marry him.

SHARING INFORMATION

Discuss these questions in pairs, in small groups, or with the whole class.

1. How does a person know that he or she is in love?
2. Kristin is 21. Is this a good age to get married? Or do you think it's better to be older?

SENTENCE COMPLETION

Complete the sentences with these words.

think	in love	look	marry

1. Gina is _____ with Larry.
2. She's going to _____ him in a month.
3. My sister is in the hospital. I _____ about her a lot.
4. Alan is 80, but he doesn't _____ old.

lucky	how	very	time

5. My computer isn't working, and I don't know _____ to fix it.
6. Erica is _____. She has a good job and good friends.
7. Do we have _____ to stop for something to eat?
8. Brandon has two houses and a lot of money in the bank. He's _____ rich.

MAKING COMPLETE SENTENCES

Draw lines from column A to column B to make complete sentences.

A	**B**
1. Do you think Brianna	looks new.
2. Your car	that you don't get sick much.
3. How do you know	is going to marry Shawn?
4. I have a big problem,	that Brett will help us?
5. You're lucky	and I often think about it.

Make complete sentences by joining the words from columns A and B.

Example

1. *Do you think Brianna is going to marry Shawn?*
2. _____
3. _____
4. _____
5. _____

I Never Forget

🎧 **WORD BANK**

1. **there is** (**there's**)   <u>*There is* a TV in the living room.</u> We use **there is** to say that something exists. **There's** is the contraction of <u>there</u> + <u>is</u>.
2. **never**   *I <u>never</u> drink coffee. I don't like it.* **Never** means at no time; not ever. **Always** is the opposite of never.
3. **forget**   *Don't <u>forget</u> to phone me.* To **forget** means not to remember something. **Remember** is the opposite of forget.
4. **next**   *What time does our <u>next</u> class begin?* **Next** means the one after the present one.
5. **get**   *Tiffany is going to the mall to <u>get</u> a dress for the party.* To **get** is to obtain or to buy something.
6. **earring**   *I like your <u>earrings</u>. They're very nice.* An **earring** is jewelry you wear on your ear.
7. **rose**   <u>*Roses*</u> *are my favorite flowers.* A **rose** is a pretty flower with a nice smell.

PREVIEW QUESTIONS

Discuss these questions before listening to and reading the dialog.

1. Do you like to eat out?
2. What do you like about eating out?

Tom Martin is talking to his friend Amanda. Tom married Kristin. She has a birthday next week. Tom is getting her earrings and roses. He's also taking her out to dinner.

Tom:	There's one thing I never forget.
Amanda:	What's that?
Tom:	Kristin's birthday. It's next week.
Amanda:	What are you getting her?
Tom:	Earrings.
Amanda:	That's nice.
Tom:	And red roses.
Amanda:	Are you taking her out to dinner?
Tom:	Yes, we're going to her favorite restaurant.

COMPREHENSION

Answer these questions about the dialog. Use your own ideas to answer the question with an asterisk.

1. What is the one thing that Tom never forgets?
2. When is Kristin's birthday?
3. What is Tom getting her?
4. What kind of flowers is he getting her?
5. Where is he taking his wife?
*6. Do you think she's happy with what Tom is doing for her birthday? Explain your answer.

SHARING INFORMATION

Discuss these questions in pairs, in small groups, or with the whole class.

1. How often do you eat out?
2. Do you have a favorite restaurant? Where is it?

SENTENCE COMPLETION

Complete the sentences with these words.

never	getting	earrings	there is

1. _____ a phone in the kitchen.
2. We are _____ a new car.
3. Paula _____ eats meat.
4. I don't like these _____. They're too big.

roses	next	forget	favorite

5. We have an English test _____ Thursday.
6. What is your _____ color?
7. Joshua is getting a dozen (12) _____ for his girlfriend.
8. Don't _____ to do your homework.

DIALOG REVIEW

Complete the paragraphs with these words.

Kristin's Birthday

forgets	earrings	there is	next

_____ one thing that Tom never _____, and that is Kristin's birthday. Her birthday is _____ week. Tom is buying her _____.

roses	getting	favorite	dinner

Tom is also _____ her red _____ and taking her out to _____. They're going to her _____ restaurant.

A Baby

WORD BANK

1. **grandmother (grandma)**   *My grandmother is 62 years old.* A **grandmother** is the mother of your mother or father.

2. **congratulations**   *Congratulations on your new job!* **Congratulations** is what we say to someone who has done something special.

3. **cute**   *Heather is in the seventh grade. She's cute.* **Cute** means pretty.

4. **weigh**   *Carl weighs 130 pounds. He's thin.* To **weigh** is to be a certain number of pounds.

5. **ounce**   *There are eight ounces of water in this glass.* An **ounce** is a small unit of weight. It is about 28 grams.

6. **pound**   *I'm going to buy 10 pounds of potatoes.* A **pound** is a unit of weight. There are 16 ounces in a pound.

7. **fine**   *"I feel fine. How are you?"* **Fine** means very good.

8. **rest**   *I'm tired. I'm going to sit down and rest.* To **rest** is to stop doing something and relax.

9. **tonight**   *Our basketball team is playing tonight.* **Tonight** is the night of today.

10. **so**   *Everyone likes Christina. She's so nice.* **So** means *very*.

PREVIEW QUESTIONS

Discuss these questions before listening to and reading the dialog.

1. How many of your grandparents are alive?
2. Where do they live?

Kristin gives birth to a girl. Her husband, Tom, is calling his mother. He tells her that the baby and mother are fine.

Tom:	Hi Grandma! Congratulations!
Grandma:	Was it a boy or a girl?
Tom:	A girl. Her name is Debra. She's cute.
Grandma:	How much does she weigh?
Tom:	Six pounds, eight ounces.
Grandma:	How's Kristin doing?
Tom:	She's fine. She's resting.
Grandma:	When can we see Debra?
Tom:	Tonight, at seven.
Grandma:	See you tonight, Tom. I'm so happy!

COMPREHENSION

Answer these questions about the dialog. Use your own ideas to answer the question with an asterisk.

1. Is the baby a boy or a girl?
2. What is the baby's name?
3. How much does she weigh?
4. How is Kristin doing?
5. When can grandma see Debra?
*6. What do grandparents do for a grandchild?

SHARING INFORMATION

Discuss these questions in pairs, in small groups, or with the whole class.

1. How often do you see your grandparents?
2. How important are (were) they in your life? Explain your answer.

SENTENCE COMPLETION

Complete the sentences with these words.

congratulations	tonight	cute	so	grandma

1. We're going to the movies _____. Do you want to come?
2. The flowers are _____ pretty.
3. I hear that you're buying a house. _____!
4. _____ takes care of the baby when I go shopping.
5. I like your dress. It's _____.

pounds	rest	weigh	fine

6. When I finish work, I go home and _____.
7. "How much do you _____?"
8. "One hundred and fifty _____."
9. Mr. Chang is a _____ teacher.

MAKING COMPLETE SENTENCES

Draw lines from column A to column B to make complete sentences.

A	**B**
1. Joan was in the hospital,	and I'm going to rest now.
2. I think that	more than I do.
3. Kate weighs 20 pounds	but she feels fine now.
4. I worked hard today,	when grandma comes to visit.
5. The children are so happy	all babies are cute.

Make complete sentences by joining the words from columns A and B.

Example

1. *Joan was in the hospital, but she feels fine now.* _____
2. _____
3. _____
4. _____
5. _____

A Student and a Cashier

Mrs. Flores
Guidance Counselor

WORD BANK

1. **guidance counselor**   *I'm going to see my <u>guidance counselor</u> to talk about what subjects I am going to take next year.* A **guidance counselor** is a person who works in a school and helps students with their problems and with what subjects to study.

2. **tell**   *Read my plan and <u>tell</u> me what you think of it.* **Tell** means to speak to someone.

3. **government**   *It is the job of the <u>government</u> to protect and help its people.* The **government** is the group of people and the laws that run a country.

4. **part-time**   *Courtney works 20 hours a week. She works <u>part-time</u>.* **Part-time** means working less than the usual number of hours. **Full-time** is usually 40 hours a week.

5. **cashier**   *Phil is a <u>cashier</u> in a clothing store.* A **cashier** is the person you pay in a store.

6. **polite**   *Kayla often says "please," "thank you," and "excuse me." She's very <u>polite</u>.* To be **polite** is to act and speak in a nice way.

7. **customer**   *Stanley buys a lot in our store. He's a good <u>customer</u>.* A **customer** is a person who buys something in a store.

36

PREVIEW QUESTIONS

Discuss these questions before listening to and reading the story.

1. Is it important to be polite to people? Why?
2. Why is it *very* important to be polite to customers?

Jackie is a high school student. She wants to go to college, but it won't be easy for her to get money to go. Her family doesn't have much money. She also has two brothers and a sister who want to go to college.

Jackie talks to Mrs. Flores, her high school guidance counselor. Mrs. Flores tells her that many students get money from the government to go to college. She helps Jackie get money from the government.

Jackie also works part-time at Staples. She works there on Saturdays and three nights a week.

Jackie is a cashier and she likes her job. She's polite to all the customers. She never forgets to say "thank you" and "have a nice day."

Jackie studies and does her homework on Sunday and before she goes to school. That's not easy, but she works because she needs the money.

COMPREHENSION

Answer these questions about the story. Use your own ideas to answer the question with an asterisk.

Paragraph 1

    1. What does Jackie want to do?
    2. Will it be easy for her to get the money to go to college? Why not?
    3. How many brothers does she have? How many sisters?

Paragraph 2

    4. Who does Jackie talk to about going to college?
    5. Where do many students get money to go to college?
  *6. Why are guidance counselors important?

Paragraph 3

    7. Where does Jackie work?
    8. What day of the week does she work?
    9. How many nights a week does she work?

Paragraph 4

  10. What is Jackie's job?
  11. Who is she polite to?
  12. What does she say to them?

Paragraph 5

  13. When does Jackie study and do her homework?
  14. Why does she work?

SHARING INFORMATION

Discuss these questions in pairs, in small groups, or with the whole class.

1. How many brothers and sisters do you have?
2. Do they live in your home country or the United States?
3. How important is it to teach young children to be polite? Explain your answer.
4. "Thank you" and "Have a nice day" are polite expressions. What are some other polite expressions?

SENTENCE COMPLETION

Complete the sentences with these words.

cashier	government	also	polite

1. There are many _____ buildings in Washington, D.C.
2. When someone says "Thank you," it's _____ to say "You're welcome."
3. I'm going to pay the _____ with my credit card.
4. I have a Toyota and my brother _____ has one.

customers	never	part-time	get

5. Many high school students work _____ after school.
6. Ben is _____ late for work.
7. You can _____ that book from the library.
8. Our store isn't making money. We need more _____.

guidance counselor	there	tell	forget

9. _____ Ashley to call me tonight.
10. When I have a problem in school, I talk to my _____.
11. Don't _____ to close the window.
12. There is a park near our house. I go _____ a lot.

A Boyfriend and a Dream

1. **same**   *Steve and I live in the <u>same</u> city.* **Same** means not different.
2. **better**   *Diego is a good soccer player, but his brother is <u>better</u>.* **Better** means of a higher quality than. Better is the comparative of good.
3. **best**   *Valerie is the <u>best</u> student in our class. She gets A's in all her subjects.* **Best** means better than all others. Best is the superlative of good.
4. **sometimes**   *<u>Sometimes</u> I walk to school; <u>sometimes</u> my mother drives me.* **Sometimes** means at times; not always.
5. **coach**   *Reggie Smith is our baseball <u>coach</u>.* A **coach** is a person who teaches and directs a team.
6. **dream**   *Charley likes to <u>dream</u> that he's very rich.* To **dream** is to think about something nice that you want to have, but that isn't easy to get.

PREVIEW QUESTIONS

Discuss these questions before listening to and reading the story.

1. Do you like to dance?
2. Are you a good dancer?

Jackie is in college now, and she has a boyfriend. His name is Pete. He goes to the same college as Jackie. On Saturday night, Jackie and Pete go to the movies or they go dancing. He's a good dancer, but Jackie is better.

Pete likes sports. He is the best player on the college basketball team. Jackie goes to his games when she can. She also likes to play basketball, and sometimes she plays with her friends in the park.

Pete wants to be a high school teacher and a basketball coach. He wants to teach history. It's his favorite subject.

Pete and Jackie are too young to get married. But Jackie likes to dream. In her dreams, she is married to Pete, has three children, a nice house, and a dog.

COMPREHENSION

Answer these questions about the story. Use your own ideas to answer the question with an asterisk.

Paragraph 1

   1. Where does Pete go to college?
   2. What do Jackie and Pete do on Saturday night?
   3. Who is the better dancer?

Paragraph 2

   4. On what team is Pete the best player?
   5. When does Jackie go to his games?
   6. Where does she play basketball?

Paragraph 3

   7. What does Pete want to be?
   8. What does he want to teach?

Paragraph 4

   9. Why don't Pete and Jackie get married now?
  10. What does Jackie like to do?
  11. In her dreams, what three things does she have?
 *12. What do you think about Jackie's dreams? Do you think she will get what she dreams about?

SHARING INFORMATION

Discuss these questions in pairs, in small groups, or with the whole class.

1. Why is it important to have a dream?
2. Do you have a dream? What is it?
3. What is your favorite dance?
4. Do you like to read about history?

SENTENCE COMPLETION

Complete the sentences with these words.

best	subject	too	team

1. Last year, our baseball _____ was very good.
2. Matt is my _____ friend. I talk to him a lot.
3. I like this coat, but it's _____ small for me.
4. I think math is a hard _____.

young	same	favorite	dream

5. Nathan and I work in the _____ store.
6. Vanessa's _____ is to be a doctor.
7. Lisa has two _____ children, Devin and Katie. He's eight and she's six.
8. This is my _____ sweater. I wear it all the time.

better	coach	sometimes	married

9. _____ Cathy and I walk to the park.
10. We have a good basketball _____. He knows how to prepare the team for a game.
11. My brother and Sue are _____, and they're going to have a baby in September.
12. Ed has a good car, but he wants a _____ one.

MATCHING

Match the words in Column A with their definitions or descriptions in Column B. Print the letters on the blank lines.

Words from the Dialogs

Column A	Column B
_____ **1.** look	**A.** a difficult situation
_____ **2.** how	**B.** to buy
_____ **3.** cute	**C.** to not remember
_____ **4.** problem	**D.** in what way
_____ **5.** never	**E.** very
_____ **6.** get	**F.** to appear to be
_____ **7.** so	**G.** at no time
_____ **8.** forget	**H.** pretty

Words from the Stories

Column A	Column B
_____ **1.** cashier	**A.** thank you; please
_____ **2.** same	**B.** they run countries
_____ **3.** tell	**C.** a person who directs a team
_____ **4.** polite	**D.** not different
_____ **5.** coach	**E.** a person who buys things
_____ **6.** sometimes	**F.** to speak to someone
_____ **7.** governments	**G.** not always
_____ **8.** customer	**H.** a person you pay

3 Families

Here are the people you will meet in the dialogs and stories in this chapter.

Jack Tina Caroline Leslie

Bobby Anne Vijay

Ricardo Elena Miguel

My Sister

WORD BANK

1. **lazy**   *Justin never does more work than he has to. He's <u>lazy</u>.* A person who is **lazy** doesn't like to work.
2. **around**   *We like to walk <u>around</u> the city.* **Around** means here and there; in different places.
3. **kid**   *When I tell people I'm 16, I'm <u>kidding</u>. I'm 30.* When people **kid**, they're not serious. To kid is to joke.
4. **only**   *There are <u>only</u> 10 students in our class.* **Only** means and no other; and no more.
5. **video games**   *Many high school students spend a lot of time playing <u>video games</u>.* **Video games** are games you play on a TV or on a screen in a game room.

PREVIEW QUESTIONS

Discuss these questions before listening to and reading the dialog.

1. How often are you lazy? Most of the time? Sometimes? Never?
2. How much work do you do around the house?

Jack and Tina are married and have three children; Caroline who's 14, Leslie who's 12, and Bobby who's two. Caroline thinks her sister is lazy. Caroline is talking to her friend Jesse.

Caroline:	My sister, Leslie, is lazy.
Jesse:	Why do you say that?
Caroline:	She doesn't do any homework.
Jesse:	Does she help around the house?
Caroline:	Are you kidding? Never.
Jesse:	How much TV does she watch?
Caroline:	Too much. She loves TV.
Jesse:	Does she play sports?
Caroline:	The only thing she plays are video games.
Jesse:	You're right. Leslie *is* lazy.

COMPREHENSION

Answer these questions about the dialog. Use your own ideas to answer the question with an asterisk.

1. Does Leslie do a lot of work?
2. How much homework does she do?
3. How often does she help around the house?
4. How much TV does she watch?
5. What games does she play?
*6. Do you think that Leslie is lazy? Explain your answer.

SHARING INFORMATION

Discuss these questions in pairs, in small groups, or with the whole class.

1. How much TV do you watch?
2. Do you ever play video games? If you do, how often?

SENTENCE COMPLETION

Complete the sentences with these words.

around	too much	lazy	never

1. Our history teacher _____ gives easy tests.
2. We pay _____ rent for this apartment. It's small.
3. I looked _____ the room for my sweater.
4. My brother won't help me paint the kitchen. He's
   _____.

kid	how much	only	video games

5. Henry's mother speaks _____ Polish.
6. I never _____ my wife about how much she
   weighs.
7. My son has to do his homework before he plays
   _____.
8. _____ did you pay for your new car?

MAKING COMPLETE SENTENCES

Draw lines from column A to column B to make complete sentences.

A	**B**
1. Frank watches TV	a video game for his birthday.
2. There are a lot of computers	because he's lazy.
3. I'm going to get Marty	only at night.
4. Jean is a very good friend,	around the school.
5. Our boss doesn't like Jerry	and I can kid her about anything.

Make complete sentences by joining the words from columns A and B.

Example

1. *Frank watches TV only at night.* _____
2. _____
3. _____
4. _____
5. _____

A Surprise

WORD BANK

1. **surprise**   *Mary is going to have twins. That's a big <u>surprise</u>.* A **surprise** is something we don't expect to happen.
2. **still**   *Is it <u>still</u> raining? Drew is <u>still</u> studying.* **Still** means continuing to.
3. **health**   *Trevor never gets sick. He has good <u>health</u>.* **Health** is the condition of your body.
4. **excellent**   *Jane is an <u>excellent</u> nurse. She's very good at helping the sick.* **Excellent** means very good.
5. **great**   *Pelé was a <u>great</u> soccer player.* **Great** means very good. Excellent and great have the same meaning.

PREVIEW QUESTIONS

Discuss these questions before listening to and reading the dialog.

1. Do you think 40 is young? Explain your answer
2. Do people who are 65 think that forty is young?

Jack will be 40 tomorrow. His wife, Tina, is having a big party for him. It's going to be a surprise. Tina is talking to her friend Ricky.

Tina:	Jack will be 40 tomorrow.
Ricky:	Are you having a party for him?
Tina:	Yes, a big one.
Ricky:	Does Jack know about it?
Tina:	No, it's going to be a surprise.
Ricky:	Jack doesn't look 40.
Tina:	You're right. He still looks and acts young.
Ricky:	And how's his health?
Tina:	Excellent.
Ricky:	That's great!

COMPREHENSION

If the sentence is true, write T. *If it's false, write* F.

_____ 1. Jack is going to be 40 tomorrow.
_____ 2. He's going to have a small party.
_____ 3. He knows about the party.
_____ 4. He looks young.
_____ 5. He gets sick a lot.

SHARING INFORMATION

Discuss these questions in pairs, in small groups, or with the whole class.

1. What's better to have—good health or a lot of money? Explain your answer.
2. What are some of the things you can do to have good health?

SENTENCE COMPLETION

Complete the sentences with these words.

surprise	still	great	tomorrow

1. Everyone likes Bonnie. She's a _____ person.
2. Is the baby _____ sleeping?
3. I'm going to the dentist _____. He's going to check my teeth.
4. We're getting Sammy a bicycle for his birthday. We want it to be a

   _____.

young	health	excellent	looks

5. Your new dress _____ pretty.
6. I go to the doctor a lot. My _____ isn't good.
7. Our new English teacher is only 22. That's _____.
8. I have a Toyota Camry. It's an _____ car.

MAKING COMPLETE SENTENCES

Draw lines from column A to column B to make complete sentences.

A	**B**
1. I often eat at this restaurant	Jan is still watching TV.
2. Not much in life is more important	to see a friend in the hospital.
3. It's 1:00 A.M. and	because the food here is excellent.
4. The president is making a surprise visit	to live in.
5. I think San Diego is a great city	than your health.

Make complete sentences by joining the words from columns A and B.

Example
1. *I often eat at this restaurant because the food here is excellent.*
2. _____
3. _____
4. _____
5. _____

A Busy Grandmother

1. **take care of**   *My wife and I are going to the movies tonight. My sister is going to <u>take care of</u> the baby*. To **take care of** is to watch someone and give the person what he or she needs.
2. **grandson**   *My <u>grandson</u> is five years old*. A **grandson** is the son of your son or daughter.
3. **keep**   *My wife and children <u>keep</u> me happy*. To **keep** is to make someone continue to be busy, happy, thin, healthy, warm, etc.
4. **busy**   *The cashier is very <u>busy</u>. A lot of people are leaving the restaurant*. **Busy** means doing something or having many things to do.
5. **try**   *Gloria weighs too much and is <u>trying</u> to lose 20 pounds*. To **try** is to make an effort to do something.

PREVIEW QUESTIONS

Discuss these questions before listening to and reading the dialog.

1. Is it easy to take care of a two-year-old baby? Explain your answer.
2. Why is it great to have a grandparent who can take care of your child?

Anne is Tina's mother. She's 65. She is going to Tina's house to take care of her grandson, Bobby. Anne is talking to her friend Vince.

Vince:	Where are you going?
Anne:	To Tina's house.
Vince:	Why?
Anne:	To take care of my grandson, Bobby.
Vince:	How old is he?
Anne:	Two. He's so cute.
Vince:	I'm sure he keeps you busy.
Anne:	Very. I love him a lot.
Vince:	You're a good grandmother.
Anne:	Thanks. I try to be.

COMPREHENSION

Answer these questions about the dialog. Use your own ideas to answer the question with an asterisk.

1. Where is Anne going?
2. Why is she going there?
3. How old is her grandson?
4. How busy is Anne?
5. What does she try to be?
*6. Do you think she likes to take care of her grandson? Explain your answer.

SHARING INFORMATION

Discuss these questions in pairs, in small groups, or with the whole class.

1. Do you think Anne is tired when she gets home from taking care of her grandson? Explain your answer.
2. If there are no grandparents to help, who can parents get to take care of their baby?

SENTENCE COMPLETION

Complete the sentences with these words.

a lot	trying	taking care of	grandsons

1. Diego and Manuela are _____ to save money to buy a house.
2. How many _____ do you have?
3. Paula is a good student and she reads _____.
4. Gabriel is very sick. His wife is _____ him.

cute	keep	so	busy

5. Joyce is a nice person. She's _____ polite.
6. Our dog is three weeks old. He's _____.
7. We're happy when our store is _____.
8. My son is trying to _____ his room clean.

DIALOG REVIEW

Complete the paragraphs with these words.

Going to Be with Bobby

grandson	house	take care of	two

Anne is going to Tina's _____. She's going to _____ Bobby, her _____. Bobby is _____.

busy	keeps	tries	cute

Bobby is so _____, but he _____ his grandmother very _____. Vince tells Anne that she's a good grandmother. Anne says she _____ to be.

The Whole Family

WORD BANK

1. **India**   *New Delhi is the capital of <u>India</u>.* **India** is a country in southern Asia.
2. **idea**   *"I have a good <u>idea</u>. Why don't we eat early and go to a movie tonight?"* An **idea** is a thought or plan.
3. **so**   *We're hungry, <u>so</u> we're going to eat lunch.* **So** means because of that.
4. **whole**   *The <u>whole</u> class is taking the test.* **Whole** means all of.
5. **stay**   *"<u>Stay</u> with us, don't go." Everyone wants to stay healthy.* To **stay** is to remain or to continue to be.
6. **together**   *Kareem and I often eat lunch <u>together</u>.* **Together** means with another person or as a group.

PREVIEW QUESTIONS

Discuss these questions before listening to and reading the dialog.

1. Do you think most people come to the United Sates to get a good job?
2. What are other reasons why people come to the United States?

Vijay is from India. It's his first day in class. He is talking to Caroline, Jack and Tina's daughter. Vijay is in Caroline's math class.

Caroline:	Where are you from, Vijay?
Vijay:	India.
Caroline:	Why did you come to the United States?
Vijay:	It was my father's idea.
Caroline:	Why did he come?
Vijay:	To get a good job.
Caroline:	Where is your mom?
Vijay:	My mom and two sisters are here, too.
Caroline:	So the whole family is here.
Vijay:	Yes, we want to stay together.

COMPREHENSION

Answer these questions about the dialog. Use your own ideas to answer the question with an asterisk.

1. Where is Vijay from?
2. Why did he come to the United States?
3. Why did his father come?
4. Where is Vijay's mom?
5. Why is the whole family here?
*6. Do you think Vijay likes living in the United States? Explain your answer.

SHARING INFORMATION

Discuss these questions in pairs, in small groups, or with the whole class.

1. Why did you come to the United States?
2. Is your whole family in the United States? If not, who is still in your home country?

SENTENCE COMPLETION

Complete the sentences with these words.

come	stay	whole	ideas

1. Randy doesn't say much, but he has a lot of great
   _____.

2. Kimberly is trying to _____ thin, but it's not easy.

3. I'm glad that Jeremy is going to _____ to the
   dance.

4. The _____ team is playing well.

job	get	together	so

5. Kate and Peggy like to study _____.

6. I work in a restaurant, but I'm looking for a better
   _____.

7. It's very cold, _____ you'll need a hat.

8. I'm going to the mall to _____ a pair of shoes.

MAKING COMPLETE SENTENCES

Draw lines from column A to column B to make complete sentences.

A	B
1. Betty is cleaning the whole house;	but she stays active.
2. Gene and Ivan are painters,	and it's going to look nice.
3. Helen is 80,	on how to get a job.
4. Ron is very rich, so he can	and they work together.
5. This book has some excellent ideas	buy anything he wants.

Make complete sentences by joining the words from columns A and B.

Example

1. *Betty is cleaning the whole house; it's going to look nice.*
2. _____
3. _____
4. _____
5. _____

From the Dominican Republic to Manhattan

HAITI

DOMINICAN
REPUBLIC

Santo Domingo

Caribbean Sea

WORD BANK

1. **town**   *Five thousand people live in our <u>town</u>.* A **town** is a very small city.
2. **the Dominican Republic**   *Santo Domingo is the capital and largest city of the <u>Dominican Republic</u>.* **The Dominican Republic** is a country in the Caribbean Sea, southeast of Florida.
3. **Manhattan**   *Many Dominicans live in <u>Manhattan</u>.* **Manhattan** is an island and part of New York City.
4. **leave**   *I <u>leave</u> my house at seven o'clock in the morning to go to work.* To **leave** is to go away from a place or person.
5. **cousin**   *My aunt has three children. They're my <u>cousins</u>.* A **cousin** is the child of your aunt or uncle.
6. **different**   *Ken is my best friend, but we're very <u>different</u>.* **Different** means not like; not the same.
7. **field**   *The park has a baseball and a soccer <u>field</u>.* A **field** is an open area of land, often used for sports.
8. **introduce**   *"Brittany, I want to <u>introduce</u> you to my friend Gail."* To **introduce** is to have someone meet another person for the first time.
9. **be (or feel) at home**   *I <u>am at home</u> in Tyler's house. He's a good friend.* To **be at home** is an expression. It means to feel the way you feel in your home, to feel relaxed.

PREVIEW QUESTIONS

Discuss these questions before listening to and reading the story.

1. Was it hard for you to leave home to come to the United States? Explain your answer.
2. Who did you come to the United States with?

It's hard for Miguel to leave home. It's hard to say good-bye to his cousins, friends, and grandparents. It's hard to leave a country and school he loves.

Miguel is leaving Tenares, a small town in the Dominican Republic. He's going to Manhattan with his mom, dad, a sister, and two brothers.

Miguel's school in Manhattan is different from his school in Tenares. It's very big. There are no fields to play on. He doesn't know anyone in his class. He doesn't know any English. He isn't happy.

His ESL teacher is friendly. She understands and wants to help Miguel. She introduces him to the class.

Six months later, Miguel likes school. He has a lot of friends. He knows some English. He knows the teachers and they know him. He's at home.

COMPREHENSION

Answer these questions about the story. Use your own ideas to answer the question with an asterisk.

Paragraph 1
1. What are three things that are hard for Miguel to leave?
2. Who is it hard for him to say good-bye to?

Paragraph 2
3. What town and country is he leaving?
4. Where is he going?
5. Who is he going with?

Paragraph 3
6. Is the school Miguel goes to in Manhattan the same as his school in Tenares?
7. How many students in his class does he know?
8. How much English does he know?

Paragraph 4
9. What is good about Miguel's ESL teacher? Name three things.
10. What does she do?

Paragraph 5
11. How does Miguel feel about school six months later?
12. How many friends does he have?
13. How much English does he know?
*14. How important is it for Miguel to make friends at school? Explain your answer.

SHARING INFORMATION

Discuss these questions in pairs, in small groups, or with the whole class.

1. What is the most difficult thing about living in the United States?
2. What is the best thing about living in the United States?
3. Do you feel more at home in the United States now than before? Explain your answer.
4. How are schools in the United States different from those in your home country?

SENTENCE COMPLETION

Complete the sentences with these words.

hard	town	cousin	field

 1. My _____ and I like to play video games.
 2. Can you help me with my homework? It's _____.
 3. The soccer team is playing on their new _____.
 4. There is only one restaurant in _____.

later	there are	friendly	introduce

 5. _____ 12 students and a teacher in the classroom.
 6. Dennis is going to _____ me to his sister.
 7. I have to go now. I'll see you _____.
 8. Everyone likes Salimah. She's very _____.

leaves	different	understand	at home

 9. When people visit us, we try to make them feel _____.
 10. Jim and Erin are _____. He's quiet and she always has something to say.
 11. Julia _____ for school at 7:30.
 12. I don't _____ your question.

Mom and Dad

WORD BANK

1. **factory**   *Curtis works in a factory that makes shoes.* A **factory** is a building where people make things.
2. **take**   *Marge takes a bus to work.* To **take** is to use a bus, taxi, train, or plane to go somewhere.
3. **subway**   *You can go to many places in New York City by subway.* A **subway** is a train that runs under the ground.
4. **low**   *I shop at stores that have low prices.* **Low** means small in amount or number.
5. **chance**   *My son has a chance to study in Italy for a year.* A **chance** is an opportunity to do something.
6. **custodian** (janitor)   *The custodians clean the classrooms every day.* A **custodian** is a person who cleans and repairs things in a building.
7. **Major Leagues**   *The New York Yankees are a Major League baseball team.* A **league** is a group of teams that play each other. The two baseball leagues with the best teams are called the **Major Leagues**.
8. **someday**   *We're going to buy a house someday.* **Someday** means at an unknown time in the future.
9. **maybe**   *"Are you going to watch TV tonight?" "Maybe, I don't know."* We use **maybe** to say that it's possible that something will happen.

62

PREVIEW QUESTIONS

Discuss these questions before listening to and reading the story.

1. How hard is it to work in a factory?
2. How much English do you have to know to work in a factory? To be a custodian?

Ricardo is Miguel's dad. He works in a factory. He takes a subway to work. His pay is low, but it's a job and he needs the money.

Elena is Miguel's mom. She works for Dr. and Mrs. Sanchez. She takes care of their three-year-old daughter, Monica. She loves Monica and Monica loves her. It's a nice job.

One day, Ricardo gets a chance for a better job. His cousin works as a custodian at George Washington High School in Manhattan. He gets Ricardo a job as a custodian. Ricardo's pay is much better than before. He can walk to work. He's very happy in his new job.

Miguel is in high school now. He goes to the school where his father works. He likes the school and he's a good student. He's also on the baseball team and he's a very good player. He dreams of playing in the Major Leagues someday. Who knows? Maybe he will.

COMPREHENSION

Answer these questions about the story. Use your own ideas to answer the question with an asterisk.

Paragraph 1

1. Where does Ricardo work?
2. How does he get to work?
3. Does he make a lot of money?

Paragraph 2

4. Who does Elena work for?
5. Who does she take care of?
6. How does she feel about Monica? How does Monica feel about her?

Paragraph 3

7. What chance does Ricardo get?
8. What job does his cousin get for him?
9. Why is Ricardo happy in his new job? Give two reasons.

Paragraph 4

10. To what school does Miguel go? Is he a good student?
11. What sport does he play?
12. What does he dream of doing someday?
*13. Do you think he has a good chance of doing what he dreams of? Explain your answer.

SHARING INFORMATION

Discuss these questions in pairs, in small groups, or with the whole class.

1. Do people often get jobs with the help of a friend or relative? Explain your answer.
2. Do you like baseball? Do or did you ever play baseball?
3. Do you ever watch baseball on TV? How often?
4. Many Major League baseball players come from the Dominican Republic. What other countries send players to the Major Leagues?

SENTENCE COMPLETION

Complete the sentences with these words.

custodian	factory	taking	maybe

1. Hillary is _____ a taxi to the airport.
2. Joe works in a _____ that makes furniture.
3. I don't know where my ring is. _____ my wife knows.
4. The _____ is fixing a student's desk.

chance	dreams	also	Major Leagues

5. Alisha is a good doctor. She's _____ very nice.
6. Schools give children a _____ to learn.
7. Only the best baseball players make it to the _____.
8. Melanie is in high school and _____ of going to college.

better	someday	subways	low

9. I try to eat food that is _____ in fat.
10. Ben wants to be rich _____.
11. Andy is a good student, but his sister is _____.
12. I like to take _____. They're fast.

MATCHING

Match the words in column A with their definitions or descriptions in column B. Print the letters on the blank lines.

Words from the Dialogs

Column A

_____ **1.** together
_____ **2.** kid
_____ **3.** excellent
_____ **4.** whole
_____ **5.** only
_____ **6.** still
_____ **7.** idea
_____ **8.** try

Column B

A. all of
B. to make an effort to
C. continuing to
D. to joke
E. a thought
F. with another person
G. and no more
H. very good

Words from the Stories

Column A

_____ **1.** cousin
_____ **2.** someday
_____ **3.** field
_____ **4.** chance
_____ **5.** maybe
_____ **6.** leave
_____ **7.** subway
_____ **8.** town

Column B

A. in the future
B. it's possible
C. a very small city
D. an open area of land
E. runs under the ground
F. an opportunity
G. a child of your aunt or uncle
H. to go away from

Jobs

Here are the people you will meet in the dialogs and stories in this chapter.

Mrs. Donato

Amy

Mark

Gino

Donna

Kevin

My Best Teacher

WORD BANK

1. **clear**   *The questions on the test were <u>clear</u>.* **Clear** means easy to understand.
2. **shout**   *"Please don't <u>shout</u> at me. I can hear very well."* To **shout** is to say something in a loud voice.
3. **kind**   *Paula is always helping other people. She's <u>kind</u>.* **Kind** means caring about others; friendly.
4. **interesting**   *This is an <u>interesting</u> book. I like it a lot.* **Interesting** means holding one's attention.

PREVIEW QUESTIONS

Discuss these questions before listening to and reading the dialog.

1. What makes someone a good teacher?
2. Do you think it's easy to be a good teacher? Explain your answer.

Chris and Megan are in high school. They're talking about Mrs. Donato, Megan's history teacher. She's Megan's best teacher.

Chris: Who's your best teacher?

Megan: My history teacher, Mrs. Donato.

Chris: What makes her so good?

Megan: She loves history.

Chris: That's important.

Megan: She's also clear.

Chris: That's good. Does she ever shout?

Megan: Never. She's very kind.

Chris: Are her classes interesting?

Megan: Very. She's the best.

COMPREHENSION

Answer these questions about the dialog. Use your own ideas to answer the question with an asterisk.

1. Who is Megan's best teacher?
2. What does she teach?
3. Is she easy to understand?
4. How often does she shout?
5. How interesting are her classes?
*6. Would you like to have Mrs. Donato for a teacher? Explain your answer.

SHARING INFORMATION

Discuss these questions in pairs, in small groups, or with the whole class.

1. Is it important for a teacher to love his or her subject? Explain your answer.
2. How important is it for a teacher to be interesting?

SENTENCE COMPLETION

Complete the sentences with these words.

clear	best	kind	never

1. Lauren is very _____. She will do anything for you.
2. Jim is rich. He stays at the _____ hotels.
3. Leslie _____ goes to the movies.
4. This is a good map of Los Angeles. It's very _____.

important	shouts	interesting	ever

5. I don't like it when my mom _____ at me.
6. Do you _____ play tennis?
7. Money isn't everything, but it's _____.
8. On Sunday night, I watch *60 Minutes*. It's an _____ TV program.

MAKING COMPLETE SENTENCES

Draw lines from column A to column B to make complete sentences.

A	B
1. It's not polite	is clear and interesting.
2. Good writing	needs to see a doctor.
3. I'm reading	to shout at people.
4. Roger is sick and	so it's easy to talk to her.
5. Our guidance counselor is kind,	an interesting story.

Make complete sentences by joining the words from columns A and B.

Example

1. *It's not polite to shout at people.* _____

2. _____

3. _____

4. _____

5. _____

A Nurse

WORD BANK

1. **become**   *Angela wants to <u>become</u> a lawyer.* To **become** means to come to be something; to start to be.
2. **wonderful**   *Bob is a <u>wonderful</u> cook.* **Wonderful** means great; very good.
3. **emergency room**   *Cindy was in an accident. They're taking her to the <u>emergency room</u> of the General Hospital.* An **emergency** is a problem that you must take care of immediately. Hospitals have **emergency rooms** for patients who need immediate care.
4. **must**   *Doug didn't eat lunch. He <u>must</u> be hungry.* **Must** is used to show that you think something is true.
5. **hope**   *I <u>hope</u> I do well on my test.* To **hope** is to want something to be true.
6. **so**   *"I think Rashad is a good doctor." "Why do you think <u>so</u>?"* **So** means that's true. It is used in place of repeating what we say.

71

PREVIEW QUESTIONS

Discuss these questions before listening to and reading the dialog.

1. Does a nurse have a difficult job? Explain your answer.
2. Does a nurse have an important job? Explain your answer.

Amy is Mrs. Donato's sister. She's a nurse at Valley Hospital. She works in the emergency room. She meets Paul at a party. They're talking.

Paul: Where do you work?

Amy: I'm a nurse at Valley Hospital.

Paul: Why did you become a nurse?

Amy: To help people.

Paul: That's wonderful!

Amy: I work in the emergency room.

Paul: You must be very busy.

Amy: Yes, most of the time.

Paul: And you help a lot of people.

Amy: I hope so.

COMPREHENSION

If the sentence is true, write T. *If it's false, write* F.

_____ 1. Amy works in a hospital.
_____ 2. She's a nurse because she wants to make a lot of money.
_____ 3. Paul thinks it's great that Amy wants to help people.
_____ 4. Amy works in an office in the hospital.
_____ 5. She's busy most of the time.

SHARING INFORMATION

Discuss these questions in pairs, in small groups, or with the whole class.

1. Which is true?
    a. A good nurse is pretty.
    b. A good nurse is kind.
    c. A good nurse is young.
2. Nurses help people. What are some other jobs in which you help people?

SENTENCE COMPLETION

Complete the sentences with these words.

nurses	wonderful	hope	busy

1. I _____ that it doesn't rain tomorrow.
2. Most _____ take good care of their patients.
3. On Saturday morning, our store is very _____.
4. Rome is a _____ city.

must	so	become	emergency room

5. Ed hopes to _____ a guidance counselor.
6. "Is Jessica coming to our party?" "I think _____."
7. Joan has to go the hospital now. Take her to the _____.
8. Scott loves his new job and his pay is good. He _____ be happy.

MAKING COMPLETE SENTENCES

Draw lines from column A to column B to make complete sentences.

A	**B**
1. We hope that we can	but I don't think so.
2. If it's an emergency,	she's very happy.
3. They say Ted is the best player on our team,	go to Mexico next year.
4. Andrea is going to become a grandmother;	a wonderful place to visit.
5. Niagara Falls is	call 911!

Make complete sentences by joining the words from columns A and B.

Example

1. *We hope that we can go to Mexico next year.* _____

2. _____

3. _____

4. _____

5. _____

A Barber

🎧 **WORD BANK**

1. **barber**   *Frank is a good <u>barber</u>. I like the way he cuts my hair.* A **barber** is a person who cuts men's hair.
2. **another**   *I'm not happy with my dentist. I'm going to go to <u>another</u> one.* **Another** means a different one; not the same.
3. **firefighter**   *The <u>firefighters</u> are getting everyone out of the building and putting out the fire.* A **firefighter** is a person who fights fires.
4. **cut**   *Tony is <u>cutting</u> his fingernails.* To **cut** is to make something shorter.
5. **free time**   *Grace has two children and a full-time job. She has very little <u>free time</u>.* **Free time** is time when you have no work to do.

PREVIEW QUESTIONS

Discuss these questions before listening to and reading the dialog.

1. Who do you think makes more money, a barber or a firefighter?
2. Does a firefighter have an important job? Explain your answer.

Mark is Mrs. Donato's brother. He's a barber. He likes his job, but he doesn't make much money. He wants to become a firefighter. He meets Emily at a friend's house.

Emily: What's your job?

Mark: I'm a barber.

Emily: Do you like your job?

Mark: Yes, but I don't make much money.

Emily: Are you looking for another job?

Mark: Yes. I want to be a firefighter.

Emily: That's good. You'll make more money.

Mark: And I can still cut hair.

Emily: How?

Mark: I can do it in my free time.

COMPREHENSION

Answer these questions about the dialog. Use your own ideas to answer the question with an asterisk.

1. What is Mark's job?
2. Does he like his job?
3. What's the problem with it?
4. What does Mark want to be?
5. How can Mark still cut hair after he becomes a firefighter?
*6. Does a firefighter have an interesting job?

SHARING INFORMATION

Discuss these questions in pairs, in small groups, or with the whole class.

1. Is it easy to be a barber? Explain your answer.
2. Is it easy to be a firefighter? Explain your answer.

SENTENCE COMPLETION

Complete the sentences with these words.

still	free time	another	barber

1. I don't like this sweater. I'm going to buy _____ one.
2. Is your daughter _____ sick?
3. I'm going to the _____ this afternoon.
4. In my _____, I like to read or watch TV.

cutting	looking for	hair	firefighter

5. A _____ has to be strong.
6. Michelle is _____ a bigger apartment.
7. Evan is _____ the grass in his yard.
8. Dan is 65. He has gray _____.

DIALOG REVIEW

Complete the paragraphs with these words.

Looking for a New Job

job	another	barber	make

Mark is a _____. He likes his _____, but he doesn't _____ much money. He's looking for _____ job.

free time	still	hair	firefighter

Mark wants to be a _____. If he can get this job, he can _____ cut _____ in his _____.

A Mechanic

WORD BANK

1. **mechanic**   *A mechanic is working on my car.* A **mechanic** is a person who fixes cars.
2. **kid**   *The kids are playing in the park.* A **kid** is a child. *Kid* is an informal word.
3. **repair**   *Our TV isn't working. We have to get someone to repair it.* To **repair** is to fix something.
4. **not yet**   *"Did you eat lunch?" "Not yet"* **Not yet** means no I didn't, but I am going to.
5. **soon**   *It's June 15. Summer will be here soon.* **Soon** means in a short time.

PREVIEW QUESTIONS

Discuss these questions before listening to and reading the dialog.

1. Does a mechanic make much money?
2. Does a mechanic have a difficult job?

Gino is from Italy. He's a mechanic. He fixes Mrs. Donato's car.

Mrs. Donato:	You're a good mechanic.
Gino:	Thanks.
Mrs. Donato:	Where did you learn to repair cars?
Gino:	In Italy, when I was a kid.
Mrs. Donato:	Are you studying English?
Gino:	Not yet.
Mrs. Donato:	When are you going to start?
Gino:	Soon.
Mrs. Donato:	Good. I can see you like your job.
Gino:	I do. I love it.

COMPREHENSION

Answer these questions about the dialog. Use your own ideas to answer the question with an asterisk.

1. What does Mrs. Donato tell Gino?
2. Where did Gino learn to repair cars?
3. Is Gino studying English?
4. When is he going to start?
5. Does he like his job?
*6. To get a job in the United States, does a mechanic have to know English?

SHARING INFORMATION

Discuss these questions in pairs, in small groups, or with the whole class.

1. Do you ever do any work on your car? Or do you leave everything to a mechanic?
2. Does a mechanic have an important job? Explain your answer.

SENTENCE COMPLETION

Complete the sentences with these words.

soon	mechanic	study	repairing

1. I can't go out tonight. I have to _____.
2. Jeff is an excellent _____. That's why he's so busy.
3. Jennifer is _____ her bike. She wants to ride it today.
4. I'm hungry. Are we going to eat dinner _____?

not yet	starts	learning	kids

5. The party _____ at eight o'clock.
6. The _____ are in the yard. They're playing basketball.
7. "Is it raining?" "_____."
8. Ahmad knows Arabic and English, and now he's _____ French.

MAKING COMPLETE SENTENCES

Draw lines from column A to column B to make complete sentences.

A	B
1. "Did you do your homework?"	my computer?
2. My son likes cars;	two boys and a girl.
3. Peter and Janet have three kids,	leave soon.
4. Can you repair	"Not yet."
5. We have to	he's going to be a mechanic.

Make complete sentences by joining the words from columns A and B.

Example

1. *"Did you do your homework?" "Not yet."* _____
2. _____
3. _____
4. _____
5. _____

A Dental Hygienist

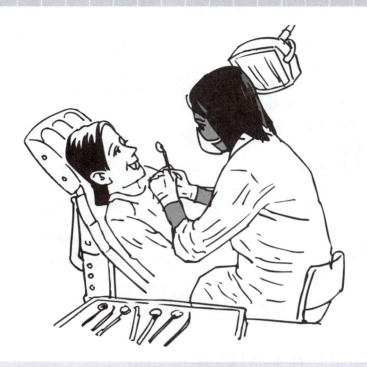

WORD BANK

1. **graduate**   *Justin is going to graduate from high school in June and enter college in September.* To **graduate** is to finish your education at a school or college.
2. **bank teller**   *Charley is giving the bank teller his check, and she is giving him cash.* A **bank teller** is the person in a bank who receives and pays out money.
3. **at first**   *At first, I didn't like Marie, but now we're in love.* **At first** means in the beginning.
4. **quit**   *I'm going to quit my job and look for another one.* To **quit** is to leave your job.
5. **dental hygienist**   *Ashley is cleaning Adam's teeth. She's a dental hygienist.* A **dental hygienist** is a person who checks and cleans your teeth.
6. **spend**   *I spend a lot of time and money at the supermarket.* To **spend** is to use time or money.
7. **beach**   *This is a great day to go to the beach. It's hot and sunny.* A **beach** is a sandy area next to an ocean or lake.
8. **picture (photograph)**   *I have a great picture of you and your wife at our party.* A **picture** is an image of someone or something.
9. **camera**   *Does your camera take good pictures?* You use a **camera** to take pictures.
10. **cost**   *The sweater costs $35.* The **cost** of something is how much money you have to pay for it.

PREVIEW QUESTIONS

Discuss these questions before listening to and reading the story.

1. Does a bank teller have an interesting job? Explain your answer.
2. Does a dental hygienist have an interesting job? Explain your answer.

Donna graduates from high school, but she doesn't want to go to college. She wants to get a job and make some money. She gets a job as a bank teller.

Donna works as a bank teller for two years. At first, everything is new and she likes her job. But that changes and she isn't happy. So she quits her job.

After she quits, Donna goes to school and studies to be a dental hygienist. She works in a dentist's office now. She cleans and checks teeth. She likes her work, and her pay is good.

In the summer, Donna spends a lot of time at the beach. She loves to swim in the ocean. She's an excellent swimmer.

Donna also likes to take pictures, and she's very good at it. She has a new camera. It costs $200 and takes good pictures.

COMPREHENSION

Answer these questions about the story. Use your own ideas to answer the question with an asterisk.

Paragraph 1

1. How does Donna feel about going to college?
2. What does she want to do?
3. What job does she get?

Paragraph 2

4. How long does Donna work as a bank teller?
5. At first, how does she feel about her job?
6. Why does she quit her job?

Paragraph 3

7. What does Donna do after she quits?
8. Where does she work now?
9. What does she do?

Paragraph 4

10. Where does Donna spend a lot of time in the summer?
11. What does she love to do?

Paragraph 5

12. What does Donna also like to do?
13. How much does her camera cost?

*14. Do you like to take pictures? Do you take a lot of them?

SHARING INFORMATION

Discuss these questions in pairs, in small groups, or with the whole class.

1. Do you think you would like to be a bank teller? Explain your answer.
2. Do you think you would like to be a dental hygienist? Explain your answer.
3. Can you swim? Do you like to swim? Do you swim much?
4. Where do you swim? Do or did you ever swim in the ocean?

SENTENCE COMPLETION

Complete the sentences with these words.

bank teller	at first	beach	quit

1. I like to sit on the _____ and look at the ocean.
2. The _____ is counting money.
3. Rebecca's pay is low. She's going to _____ her job.
4. _____ I didn't understand our math homework, but now I do.

camera	costs	dental hygienist	change

5. That dress _____ $100.
6. This isn't a good plan. We have to _____ it.
7. It's very easy to take pictures with this _____.
8. Rosa wants to be a _____.

graduate	pictures	spend	excellent

9. This is an _____ computer. I like it.
10. I want to show you some _____ of the baby.
11. We _____ a lot of money at the mall.
12. Karen is going to _____ from college next year.

A Salesperson

WORD BANK

1. **special**   *Today is my 50th birthday. It's a special day.* **Special** means very important.
2. **handsome**   *Jack is handsome, and his wife is beautiful.* **Handsome** means good-looking. Handsome is a word we use when talking about a man.
3. **sell**   *Supermarkets sell food.* To **sell** is to give something and get money for it.
4. **salesperson**   *Lindsay sells books. She's a salesperson.* A **salesperson** is a person who sells something.
5. **frequently**   *I visit my friend frequently.* **Frequently** means happening often.
6. **drum**   *Tony loves music and he plays the drums.* A **drum** is a musical instrument.
7. **band**   *The band that played at the dance was very good.* A **band** is a group of people who play music.
8. **wedding**   *Kathy and Dave are getting married tomorrow. It's going to be a big wedding.* A **wedding** is the ceremony at which a man and woman marry.
9. **expensive**   *My new car is expensive. It costs $30,000.* **Expensive** means costing a lot of money.

PREVIEW QUESTIONS

Discuss these questions before listening to and reading the story.

1. Would you like to be a salesperson? Explain your answer.
2. Do you think it's important for a car salesperson to be very interested in cars? Explain your answer.

Donna is very friendly. She likes to go to parties, and she has a lot of friends. But she has one special friend. His name is Kevin. He's tall and handsome, and he's 25 years old.

Kevin is a car salesperson. He works for Toyota and is very good at selling cars. He loves cars and knows a lot about them.

Kevin is a good swimmer and frequently goes swimming with Donna. He also likes music a lot. He plays the drums in a small band. The band plays at parties and weddings.

Donna and Kevin are in love. They're going to get married in June. They love to eat out and to talk. They talk about their jobs, their friends, and their future.

Kevin and Donna hope to buy a house after they get married. That won't be easy. Houses are expensive.

COMPREHENSION

Answer these questions about the story. Use your own ideas to answer the question with an asterisk.

Paragraph 1

    1. Where does Donna like to go?
    2. What's the name of her special friend?
    3. Is he handsome? How old is he?

Paragraph 2

    4. What is Kevin's job?
    5. What company does he work for?
    6. What does he love and know a lot about?

Paragraph 3

    7. Who does Kevin go swimming with? How often?
    8. What musical instrument does he play?
    9. Where does his band play?

Paragraph 4

    10. When are Kevin and Donna going to get married?
  *11. Why do you think that so many people get married in June?
    12. What do Kevin and Donna talk about when they eat out?

Paragraph 5

    13. What do Kevin and Donna hope to buy after they get married?
    14. Why will that be difficult?

SHARING INFORMATION

Discuss these questions in pairs, in small groups, or with the whole class.

1. Do you think that Toyota makes good cars?
2. Kevin is very interested in cars. Are you?
3. Do you have a car?
4. If you do, tell us about it.

SENTENCE COMPLETION

Complete the sentences with these words.

wedding	handsome	salesperson	hope

1. Carol likes Alan. He's _____ and very nice.
2. Melissa is a _____ for a large computer company.
3. Kim's _____ dress is very pretty.
4. I _____ my son gets a job soon.

a lot of	special	drums	sell

5. Where did Greg learn to play the _____? He plays them well.
6. _____ people weigh too much.
7. Nick and Laura are going to _____ their house and move to California.
8. Mary Beth is a _____ person. She's very kind, polite, and smart.

band	expensive	frequently	in love

9. Brenda and Bill go out together a lot. I think they're

   _____.
10. We don't stay at _____ hotels.
11. The_____ is playing my favorite song.
12. I _____ call my mom and dad.

MATCHING

Match the words in column A with their definitions or descriptions in column B. Print the letters on the blank lines.

Words from the Dialogs

Column A	Column B
_____ **1.** clear	**A.** a different one
_____ **2.** kid	**B.** to fix
_____ **3.** another	**C.** a person who cuts hair
_____ **4.** soon	**D.** easy to understand
_____ **5.** repair	**E.** great
_____ **6.** kind	**F.** in a short time
_____ **7.** barber	**G.** a child
_____ **8.** wonderful	**H.** caring about others

Words from the Stories

Column A	Column B
_____ **1.** spend	**A.** a sandy area next to an ocean
_____ **2.** handsome	**B.** happening often
_____ **3.** beach	**C.** to leave a job
_____ **4.** special	**D.** costing a lot
_____ **5.** quit	**E.** very important
_____ **6.** at first	**F.** to use time or money
_____ **7.** frequently	**G.** in the beginning
_____ **8.** expensive	**H.** good-looking

5 Exercise and Sports

Here are the people you will meet in the dialogs and stories in this chapter.

John

Kelly

Brad

Tim

Laura

Tommy

Diana

Swimming

WORD BANK

1. **vacation**   *When I'm on <u>vacation</u>, I don't think about my job.* A **vacation** is time away from work or school.
2. **lake**   *It's too cold to swim in the <u>lake</u>.* A **lake** is a large body of water with land around it.
3. **far**   *New York is <u>far</u> from California.* **Far** means a long distance.
4. **about**   *I weigh <u>about</u> 140 pounds.* **About** means a little more or a little less than.
5. **mile**   *It's 300 <u>miles</u> from Philadelphia to Boston.* A **mile** is a distance of 5,280 feet, or 1.6 kilometers.
6. **of course**   *<u>Of course</u> children like to play.* **Of course** is an expression. It means certainly.

PREVIEW QUESTIONS

Discuss these questions before listening to and reading the dialog.

1. Where did you go on your last vacation?
2. What did you do on your last vacation?

John and his sister, Kelly, are going on a vacation. They're renting a house in the country. The house isn't far from a lake. John and Kelly like to swim.

John: We're going to have a great vacation.

Kelly: I hope so.

John: I'm going for a swim.

Kelly: Where?

John: In a small lake.

Kelly: How far is it?

John: About a mile. Do you want to come?

Kelly: Of course.

John: It has a nice beach.

Kelly: That's great.

COMPREHENSION

Answer these questions about the dialog. Use your own ideas to answer the question with an asterisk.

1. What does Kelly hope?
2. Where is John going to swim?
3. How far is it?
4. Does Kelly want to come?
5. What does the lake have?
*6. Why is it good for a lake to have a nice beach?

SHARING INFORMATION

Discuss these questions in pairs, in small groups, or with the whole class.

1. Why is it good to know how to swim?
2. If you can swim, how did you learn?

SENTENCE COMPLETION

Complete the sentences with these words.

far	of course	lake	so

1. "Is Dan going to the game?" "I think _____."
2. _____ good health is important.
3. How _____ is it from here to the post office?
4. There are a lot of boats on the _____.

vacation	beach	miles	about

5. It's two _____ from my house to school.
6. I'm very tired. I need a _____.
7. This dress costs _____ $60.
8. We like to go to the _____ in the summer.

MAKING COMPLETE SENTENCES

Draw lines from column A to column B to make complete sentences.

A	**B**
1. Is it far	five miles long.
2. The lake is	use my phone.
3. We had a	about seven o'clock.
4. Of course you can	to the park?
5. I leave for work at	wonderful vacation.

Make complete sentences by joining the words from columns A and B.

Example

1. *Is it far to the park?* _____
2. _____
3. _____
4. _____
5. _____

Tennis

WORD BANK

1. **me too**   *"I'm tired." "Me too. I'm going to rest."* **Me too** is an expression. It means, "I am too." or "I do too."

2. **near**   *We live near the park. We can walk there in five minutes.* **Near** means not far from; close to.

3. **let's = let us**   *Let's go out for dinner.* We use **let's** to ask someone to do something with us.

4. **fun**   *Everyone had fun at the party.* **Fun** means a good time; pleasure.

5. **especially**   *Karen loves ice cream, especially vanilla ice cream.* **Especially** means most of all.

6. **win**   *I hope our team wins the game.* To **win** is to score more points than the person or team you are playing against.

7. **doubt**   *I doubt that Brittany will go to school today. She's not feeling well.* To **doubt** is to think that something is not going to happen.

PREVIEW QUESTIONS

Discuss these questions before listening to and reading the dialog.

1. Do you ever play tennis?
2. Do you ever watch it on TV?

Kelly and John are on vacation. They love to play tennis. It's a lot of fun. Kelly is a better tennis player than John, but he says he's going to win this time.

Kelly: I love to play tennis.

John: Me too. It's a great sport.

Kelly: Where can we play?

John: At a park near here.

Kelly: Good. Let's go after lunch.

John: OK. Tennis is a lot of fun.

Kelly: Especially if you win.

John: And I'm going to win this time.

Kelly: I doubt it.

John: We'll see.

COMPREHENSION

If the sentence is true, write T. *If it's false, write* F.

_____ 1. Kelly and John like to play tennis.
_____ 2. They're going to play before lunch.
_____ 3. They're going to play in a park.
_____ 4. John says he's going to win.
_____ 5. Kelly also thinks he will win.

SHARING INFORMATION

Discuss these questions in pairs, in small groups, or with the whole class.

1. Do you think it's easy to learn to play tennis? Explain your answer.
2. Do many people in your home country play tennis?

SENTENCE COMPLETION

Complete the sentences with these words.

near	fun	doubt	me too

1. We like to dance. It's _____.
2. "I want to go to college." "_____."
3. Is there a supermarket _____ here?
4. I _____ I'll pass the test. I didn't study for it.

let's	especially	winning	great

5. With a minute to play, our basketball team is _____ by 10 points.
6. _____ have a picnic next Saturday.
7. Abraham Lincoln was a _____ president.
8. I like animals, _____ dogs.

MAKING COMPLETE SENTENCES

Draw lines from column A to column B to make complete sentences.

A	**B**
1. I doubt that	near our school.
2. There is a baseball field	play video games.
3. It's fun to	it will rain today.
4. Let's rent a DVD	win the big game?
5. Did our baseball team	and watch a movie.

Make complete sentences by joining the words from columns A and B.

Example

1. *I doubt that it will rain today.*_____
2. _____
3. _____
4. _____
5. _____

Going for a Walk

🎧 WORD BANK

1. **weather**   *I hope we have nice <u>weather</u> for our trip*. Sometimes our **weather** is cold, and sometimes it's hot. Sometimes our **weather** is sunny, and sometimes it's rainy.

2. **perfect**   *Your plan is good, but it's not <u>perfect</u>. There are some problems with it*. **Perfect** means the best possible.

3. **fresh air**   *I'm going out to get some <u>fresh air</u>*. **Fresh air** is air that is cool and clean.

4. **exercise**   *Running is very good <u>exercise</u>*. **Exercise** is physical activity that keeps our bodies strong and healthy.

5. **wow**   <u>*Wow*</u>*! That watch costs a thousand dollars*. **Wow** is an expression we use to show surprise.

6. **be back**   *I'm leaving, but I'll <u>be back</u> in 10 minutes*. **Be back** means to return to the place where you were before.

96

PREVIEW QUESTIONS

Discuss these questions before listening to and reading the dialog.

1. Do you walk much?
2. Where do you walk?

Yesterday it rained. Today the weather is perfect. John wants to go for a walk. Kelly thinks that's a good idea.

Kelly: The weather is perfect.

John: Let's go for a walk.

Kelly: Good idea! We can use some fresh air.

John: And exercise.

Kelly: Yes, walking is good for your heart.

John: That's right.

Kelly: Where do you want to go?

John: To the lake.

Kelly: Wow! That's far.

John: It's not that far. We'll be back in 40 minutes.

COMPREHENSION

Answer these questions about the dialog. Use your own ideas to answer the question with an asterisk.

1. What does Kelly say about the weather?
2. What does John want to do?
3. What can Kelly and John use?
4. Where does John want to go?
5. How long will it take John and Kelly to go and get back?
*6. John and Kelly are going to walk two miles. Is that a long walk?

SHARING INFORMATION

Discuss these questions in pairs, in small groups, or with the whole class.

1. How do you feel after a walk?
2. Why is walking good for the heart?

SENTENCE COMPLETION

Complete the sentences with these words.

perfect	exercise	let's	weather

1. I don't like winter and cold _____.
2. The doctor wants me to get more _____.
3. To get 95 on a test is very good, but it's not _____.
4. I'm tired. _____ go home.

wow	fresh air	be back	far

5. Brian is flying to Chicago, but he'll _____ in two days.
6. "Joan is trying to lose 50 pounds." "_____. That's a lot."
7. How _____ is it from your house to the hospital?
8. It's good for the kids to go out and play in the _____.

DIALOG REVIEW

Complete the paragraphs with these words.

A Long Walk

fresh air	weather	exercise	perfect

The _____ today is _____. John and Kelly are going for a walk. They want to get some _____ and _____.

wow	be back	far	lake

John wants to walk to the _____. Kelly says, "_____" because she thinks that's _____ to walk. John says they'll _____ in 40 minutes.

Football and Soccer

🎧

WORD BANK

1. **football**   *Our high school <u>football</u> team is playing an important game this Saturday.* **Football** is a sport in which a team tries to advance a football by running with or throwing it.

2. **exciting**   *The basketball game is very <u>exciting</u>. Our team is winning by one point, 72–71.* Something that is **exciting** makes you feel very happy or very interested.

3. **dangerous**   *Driving very fast is <u>dangerous</u>.* Anything that can easily hurt someone is **dangerous**.

4. **safe**   *Golf is a <u>safe</u> sport.* Anything that doesn't hurt anyone is **safe**.

5. **popular**   *Courtney is very <u>popular</u>. Everyone likes her.* **Popular** means liked by many people.

PREVIEW QUESTIONS

Discuss these questions before listening to and reading the dialog.

1. What is the most popular sport in your home country?
2. What do you think is the most popular sport in the United States?

Kelly is talking to her friend Brad at a party. Brad's favorite sport is football. Kelly's favorite sport is soccer.

Kelly: What's your favorite sport?

Brad: Football. It's exciting.

Kelly: I don't like football. It's too dangerous.

Brad: It's not that dangerous. What's your favorite sport?

Kelly: Soccer. It's exciting *and* safe.

Brad: True.

Kelly: It's also the most popular sport in the world.

Brad: But not in the United States.

Kelly: Someday it's going to be.

Brad: Maybe. Who knows?

COMPREHENSION

Answer these questions about the dialog. Use your own ideas to answer the question with an asterisk.

1. What is Brad's favorite sport?
2. Why doesn't Kelly like football?
3. What is her favorite sport?
4. Why is it her favorite?
5. What is the most popular sport in the world?
*6. Why do you think it's the most popular sport in the world?

SHARING INFORMATION

Discuss these questions in pairs, in small groups, or with the whole class.

1. Football is dangerous. How would you feel if your son wanted to play football?
2. Do you think that someday soccer will be the most popular sport in the United States? Explain your answer.

SENTENCE COMPLETION

Complete the sentences with these words.

exciting	someday	too	soccer

1. I'm not going to buy that camera. It's _____ expensive.
2. Our trip to Washington, D.C., was _____.
3. Italy has very good _____ teams.
4. We want to visit Russia _____.

dangerous	football	popular	safe

5. Our dog is friendly. It's _____ to play with him.
6. In the fall I like to watch _____ on TV.
7. It's _____ to be a police officer.
8. Pizza is _____ in the United States.

MAKING COMPLETE SENTENCES

Draw lines from column A to column B to make complete sentences.

A	**B**
1. My brothers	to swim alone.
2. I like to go to	football is a very popular sport.
3. It's dangerous	exciting movies.
4. The park near our house	like to play soccer.
5. In the United States	is safe.

Make complete sentences by joining the words from columns A and B.

Example

1. *My brothers like to play soccer.* _____
2. _____
3. _____
4. _____
5. _____

Alike and Different

WORD BANK

1. **way**   *I like the <u>way</u> that Mr. Kaminski teaches math.* **Way** means how a person does something.
2. **alike**   *Vicky and her sister look <u>alike</u>.* **Alike** means almost the same.
3. **both**   *Erik and his brother are lawyers, and <u>both</u> are rich.* **Both** means the two of them.
4. **angry**   *I get <u>angry</u> when my son doesn't do what I ask him.* **Angry** means feeling anger. **Anger** is a strong feeling you get when someone offends you.
5. **quickly**   *Alex works <u>quickly</u> and does a lot.* **Quickly** means in a short time; fast.
6. **rarely**   *I watch a lot of TV, but I <u>rarely</u> go to the movies.* **Rarely** means not very often.
7. **heavy**   *Vanessa is <u>heavy</u>. She weighs 200 pounds.* **Heavy** means weighing a lot.
8. **magazine**   *Sam is reading* Time, *his favorite <u>magazine</u>.* A **magazine** is a weekly or monthly publication with news and other stories. *Readers Digest, Time, Sports Illustrated*, and *Vanidades* are magazines.

PREVIEW QUESTIONS

Discuss these questions before listening to and reading the story.

1. How often do you get angry? Frequently? Sometimes? Rarely?
2. Do you think you talk more than most people do?

Tim and Laura are married and have two children. In some ways, Tim and Laura are alike and in some ways, they're very different.

Both Tim and Laura like to talk and have a lot of friends, but Tim gets angry quickly. Laura rarely gets angry.

Laura is a very healthy eater. She eats a lot of fish, fruit, and vegetables. She never eats meat. She's tall and thin.

Tim loves to eat meat, and cheeseburgers are his favorite food. He rarely eats vegetables, but he does eat a lot of fruit. He's heavy.

Laura likes to read, and she goes to the library a lot. Tim rarely goes to the library, but he also likes to read. Laura and Tim especially like to read books and magazines about sports.

COMPREHENSION

Answer these questions about the story. Use your own ideas to answer the question with an asterisk.

Paragraph 1

    1. How many children do Tim and Laura have?

    2. How are Tim and Laura alike? How are they different?

   *3. Do you think that most husbands and wives are alike and also very different? Explain your answer.

Paragraph 2

    4. What do Tim and Laura like to do?

    5. How are they different?

Paragraph 3

    6. What does Laura eat a lot of?

    7. What does she never eat?

Paragraph 4

    8. What is Tim's favorite food?

    9. What does he rarely eat?

Paragraph 5

   10. How often does Laura go to the library?

   11. How often does Tim go?

   12. What do Tim and Laura especially like to read?

SHARING INFORMATION

Discuss these questions in pairs, in small groups, or with the whole class.

    1. What is your favorite food?

    2. What other foods do you like a lot?

    3. Do you read much? What do you like to read?

    4. How often do you go to the library? Often? Sometimes? Never?

SENTENCE COMPLETION

Complete the sentences with these words.

both	rarely	healthy	library

1. My husband _____ cooks.
2. The _____ is getting 10 new computers.
3. _____ Jeff and Tiffany are excellent students.
4. The doctor says our baby is _____. We're very happy.

alike	especially	quickly	way

5. Call 911! The police will come _____.
6. The restaurant is busy, _____ on Friday and Saturday nights.
7. There is no _____ I can help you now. I have to go to work.
8. My cousin and I are _____. We're both friendly and like to do the same things.

magazine	heavy	also	angry

9. Tyler plays the piano. He's _____ a good singer.
10. Sue gets _____ when her husband drives too fast.
11. This box is _____. What's in it?
12. I'm going to buy a _____ to read on the train.

A Sports Family

WORD BANK

1. **star**   *Roberto Clemente was a baseball <u>star</u>.* A **star** is a player or actor that many people know and like.
2. **reporter**   *Ray is a good writer and he wants to be a newspaper <u>reporter</u>.* A **reporter** is a person who writes about events for a newspaper or talks about them on TV.
3. **local**   *Janet lives at home and goes to a <u>local</u> college.* **Local** means in an area that is near.
4. **crazy about**   *Ryan is <u>crazy about</u> Emily, and she's <u>crazy about</u> him. They're going to get married next month.* **Crazy about** is an expression. It means to love a lot.
5. **lesson**   *Chelsea is taking piano <u>lessons</u>.* A **lesson** is a class; a period of time in which you learn something.
6. **twice**   *The dentist checks my teeth <u>twice</u> a year.* **Twice** means two times.
7. **junior**   *In September, Diego is going to be a <u>junior</u>.* A **junior** is a student in the third year of high school or college.
8. **like**   *Ted looks and acts <u>like</u> his father.* **Like** means similar to someone or something.

PREVIEW QUESTIONS

Discuss these questions before listening to and reading the story.

1. Do you like basketball? Do you ever watch it on TV?
2. Do or did you ever play basketball?

Laura was a basketball star in high school and college. Now, she coaches the women's basketball team at a college in Boston. She's a good coach, and her team wins most of its games.

Tim is a sports reporter for a local newspaper. It's a great job for him. He's crazy about sports and was a very good football player in high school.

Tim and Laura have two children, Tommy and Diana. Tommy is in the first grade and is a good student. He does well in all his subjects. He also takes swimming lessons twice a week.

Diana is a junior in high school. She's a lot like her mother. She's the best player on the high school basketball team and one of the best players in the state. She's tall and thin. She hopes to play basketball in college.

COMPREHENSION

Answer these questions about the story. Use your own ideas to answer the question with an asterisk.

Paragraph 1

1. What sport did Laura play in high school and college?
2. What is her job now?
3. How does her team do?

Paragraph 2

4. What is Tim's job?
5. How does he feel about sports?
6. What sport did he play in high school?

Paragraph 3

7. How many children do Tim and Laura have? What are their names?
8. How does Tommy do in school?
9. What does he take twice a week?

Paragraph 4

10. Who is Diana like?
11. In what sport is she a star?
*12. Why is it good for a basketball player to be tall?
13. What does Diana hope to do in college?

SHARING INFORMATION

Discuss these questions in pairs, in small groups, or with the whole class.

1. Why is it difficult to be a coach?
2. Is basketball a popular sport in your home country?
3. Do you ever read the sports section of the newspaper?
4. If so, what sport(s) do you like to read about?

SENTENCE COMPLETION

Complete the sentences with these words.

star	hope	win	like

1. Your house looks a lot _____ ours.
2. I _____ you can come to our party.
3. Juan is the best soccer player in the league. He's a

   _____ .

4. We're playing a very good football team today. It's going to be a hard
   game to _____ .

reporters	lessons	twice	coach

5. My daughter is 17. She's taking driving _____.
6. The basketball players like their new _____. He
   knows a lot about basketball.
7. I like to watch the news on Channel 4. They have good

   _____.

8. Jackie phoned me _____ yesterday, but I wasn't
   home.

junior	crazy about	local	subject

9. The people of Brazil are _____ soccer.
10 Ann is only a _____, but she knows where she
   wants to go to college.
11. History is an interesting _____.
12. Many of our _____ restaurants are very good.

MATCHING

Match the words in column A with their definitions or descriptions in column B. Print the letters on the blank lines.

Words from the Dialogs

Column A	Column B
_____ 1. perfect	**A.** liked by many
_____ 2. of course	**B.** won't hurt anyone
_____ 3. popular	**C.** physical activity
_____ 4. exercise	**D.** close to
_____ 5. dangerous	**E.** the best possible
_____ 6. near	**F.** a good time
_____ 7. fun	**G.** can easily hurt someone
_____ 8. safe	**H.** certainly

Words from the Stories

Column A	Column B
_____ 1. crazy about	**A.** fast
_____ 2. heavy	**B.** the two of them
_____ 3. twice	**C.** to love very much
_____ 4. quickly	**D.** an area that is near
_____ 5. alike	**E.** two times
_____ 6. both	**F.** not often
_____ 7. local	**G.** weighing a lot
_____ 8. rarely	**H.** almost the same

6 Learning

Here are the people you will meet in the dialogs and stories in this chapter.

Ravi

Anish

Maya

Malini

David Jackson

Linda Jackson

Eddie Jackson

Sara Jackson

Applying to College

WORD BANK

1. **senior**   *Carolyn is a <u>senior</u>. She's going to graduate in June.* A **senior** is a student in the fourth and last year of high school or college.
2. **apply**   *Andy is <u>applying</u> for a job.* To **apply** is to formally ask for something, usually in writing.
3. **at least**   *The car I want will cost <u>at least</u> $25,000.* **At least** means maybe more but not less; a minimum of.
4. **accept**   *A friend offers Alex $75 for his bicycle, and Alex <u>accepts</u> it.* To **accept** is to take what is offered.
5. **probably**   *It'll <u>probably</u> rain tomorrow.* **Probably** means without much doubt.
6. **grade**   *Audrey is getting an A in history. She always gets good <u>grades</u> in school.* A **grade** is a letter or number that tells how well you are doing in a subject.

PREVIEW QUESTIONS

Discuss these questions before listening to and reading the dialog.

1. What big decision do high school seniors have to make?
2. Why is it good to go to college if you can?

Ravi meets Shanta at a party. They're high school students. Ravi is a senior, and he's going to apply to college soon.

Shanta:	Where do you go to school?
Ravi:	I'm a senior at Jefferson High School.
Shanta:	Are you going to college?
Ravi:	Yes. I have to apply soon.
Shanta:	How many colleges are you applying to?
Ravi:	At least three.
Shanta:	I hope they accept you.
Ravi:	They probably will.
Shanta:	Why do you say that?
Ravi:	I have good grades.

COMPREHENSION

Answer these questions about the dialog. Use your own ideas to answer the question with an asterisk.

1. What school does Ravi go to?
2. What does he have to do soon?
3. How many colleges is he applying to?
4. What does Shanta hope?
5. Why does Ravi think the colleges will accept him?
*6. Why do you think Ravi is applying to three colleges?

SHARING INFORMATION

Discuss these questions in pairs, in small groups, or with the whole class.

1. Not everyone who graduates from high school goes to college. Why not?
2. Name some jobs you can get only if you graduate from college.

SENTENCE COMPLETION

Complete the sentences with these words.

accepts	senior	probably	grades

1. Kimberly studies a lot. She wants good _____.
2. Rachel is a _____. This is her fourth year at Lincoln High School.
3. Bill offers to help Mark paint his apartment. Mark _____ his offer.
4. We will _____ eat out tonight.

have to	at least	applying	soon

5. We're looking for an apartment that has _____ two bedrooms.
6. Jason will be home from work _____.
7. I _____ wash my hands before I eat dinner.
8. Ling wants to study in the United States. She's _____ for a visa.

MAKING COMPLETE SENTENCES

Draw lines from column A to column B to make complete sentences.

A	**B**
1. I'm not happy with my grades;	to the post office.
2. It's at least a mile	and I'm going to accept it.
3. Danielle and Corey will probably	a credit card.
4. Marie is applying for	they're very low.
5. The company is offering me a job,	get married next year.

Make complete sentences by joining the words from columns A and B.

Example

1. ***I'm not happy with my grades; they're very low.*** _____
2. _____
3. _____
4. _____
5. _____

Band Practice

WORD BANK

1. **practice**   *You need a lot of practice to learn a language.* **Practice** is doing something many times to get better at doing it.
2. **trumpet**   *Victor plays the trumpet very well.* A **trumpet** is a musical instrument that you blow into.
3. **around**   *The watch costs around $100.* **Around** means close to; about.
4. **concert**   *We're going to a concert tonight. We like music.* At a **concert**, a group plays music for many people.
5. **enjoy**   *The children enjoy playing in the park.* To **enjoy** is to like something.

PREVIEW QUESTIONS

Discuss these questions before listening to and reading the dialog.

1. Do you like to listen to music? Do you listen to it a lot?
2. What type of music do you listen to?

Vanessa and Anish are in the eighth grade. Anish is Ravi's brother. Anish has band practice after school. He is talking to Vanessa. They're in the same class.

Vanessa: What are you doing after school?

Anish: I have band practice.

Vanessa: What do you play?

Anish: The trumpet.

Vanessa: How long is practice?

Anish: Around three hours.

Vanessa: Wow! That's long.

Anish: We have a concert next week.

Vanessa: Can I come?

Anish: Sure. You'll enjoy it!

COMPREHENSION

If the sentence is true, write T. *If it's false, write* F.

_____ 1. Anish has baseball practice after school.
_____ 2. He plays the trumpet.
_____ 3. He's going to practice for five hours.
_____ 4. He has a concert next week.
_____ 5. Vanessa wants to go to the concert.

SHARING INFORMATION

Discuss these questions in pairs, in small groups, or with the whole class.

1. Do you have a favorite musical instrument? If you do, what is it?
2. Do you play a musical instrument? If you do, which one?

SENTENCE COMPLETION

Complete the sentences with these words.

play	long	enjoys	trumpet

1. Our history teacher gives _____ tests.
2. My son wants to take _____ lessons.
3. We are looking for a band to _____ at our dance.
4. Dorothy _____ reading the newspaper after breakfast.

around	concert	practice	next

5. We _____ soccer ever day after school.
6. They're going to have a _____ in the park Friday night.
7. _____ Wednesday, Mario is going to graduate from high school.
8. We eat dinner _____ six o'clock.

MAKING COMPLETE SENTENCES

Draw lines from column A to column B to make complete sentences.

A	**B**
1. I'm going to buy	to play the piano well.
2. You have to practice a lot	going to the beach.
3. What time is	800 students in our school.
4. There are around	a trumpet.
5. We enjoy	the concert tonight?

Make complete sentences by joining the words from columns A and B.

Example

1. *I'm going to buy a trumpet.* _____
2. _____
3. _____
4. _____
5. _____

A Morning Person

WORD BANK

1. **get up**   *I get up at seven o'clock every morning.* To **get up** is to get out of bed after sleeping.
2. **shower**   *After the game, the players shower and go home.* To **shower** is to stand under running water and wash yourself.
3. **then**   *When Dawn comes home from work, she reads and listens to music. Then she cooks dinner.* **Then** means after that; next.
4. **have got to**   *I have got to e-mail my friend.* **Have got to** means have to; be necessary. (I've got to = I have got to)
5. **morning person**   *Jane works much better in the morning than in the afternoon. She's a morning person.* A **morning person** is a person who does his or her best work in the morning.

PREVIEW QUESTIONS

Discuss these questions before listening to and reading the dialog.

1. What time do you get up?
2. Is it hard for you to get up in the morning?

Ravi is talking to Maya. They're cousins. Ravi gets up early to study. He's too tired to study at night.

Maya: What time do you get up?

Ravi: Five-thirty.

Maya: Why so early?

Ravi: First, I have to shower and eat breakfast.

Maya: Then what?

Ravi: I've got to study and do my homework.

Maya: Why don't you study after dinner?

Ravi: I'm too tired.

Maya: Do you ever study at night?

Ravi: No. I'm a morning person.

COMPREHENSION

Answer these questions about the dialog. Use your own ideas to answer the question with an asterisk.

1. What time does Ravi get up?
2. What does he do first when he gets up?
3. What does he do after that?
4. Why doesn't he study after dinner?
5. Does he ever study at night?
*6. Do you think Ravi goes to bed early? Explain your answer.

SHARING INFORMATION

Discuss these questions in pairs, in small groups, or with the whole class.

1. Do you usually study at night or in the morning?
2. Are you a morning person? If not, when do you do your best work?

SENTENCE COMPLETION

Complete the sentences with these words.

shower	then	have got to	too

1. These clothes are dirty. I _____ wash them.
2. I always feel better after I _____.
3. This apartment is _____ small for us.
4. After dinner, Joe does his homework. _____ he watches TV.

get up	so	morning person	ever

5. Do you _____ visit your cousins?
6. We usually _____ late on Saturdays.
7. I do my best work at night, but my wife is a _____.
8. Your son is getting _____ big.

DIALOG REVIEW

Complete the paragraphs with these words.

Ravi Gets Up Early to Study

showers	has got to	gets up	then

Ravi _____ at 5:30. First, he _____ and eats breakfast. _____ he _____ study and do his homework.

night	never	morning person	tired

Ravi is too _____ to study after dinner. He _____ studies at _____. He's a _____.

Sesame Street™

WORD BANK

1. **news**   *After dinner, I usually watch the <u>news</u> on TV.* The **news** is a report on what is happening in the world.

2. *Sesame Street*   *My kids love to watch <u>Sesame Street</u>. Sesame Street* is a very popular TV show for children.

3. **should**   *Children <u>should</u> listen to their parents and do what they tell them.* **Should** means that something is the right thing to do; that something is a good idea.

4. **definitely**   *Phil weighs 300 pounds. He <u>definitely</u> weighs too much.* **Definitely** means certainly; without doubt.

5. **lose**   *Greg is <u>losing</u> his hair.* To **lose** is to have less of something than before.

6. **improve**   *Brenda's health is <u>improving</u>. She will be able to leave the hospital soon.* To **improve** is to get better.

PREVIEW QUESTIONS

Discuss these questions before listening to and reading the dialog.

1. Do you ever watch *Sesame Street*? If so, do you like it?
2. Do you ever watch the news? Does it help you learn English?

Malini is Anish and Ravi's mother. She is studying ESL at a night school for adults. She is talking to Kedar after class. They know some English, but not a lot.

Malini: What's your favorite TV program?
Kedar: The six o'clock news, but it's hard to understand.
Malini: *Sesame Street* is my favorite.
Kedar: Isn't that for kids?
Malini: Yes. That's why it's so easy to understand.
Kedar: Hmm. Maybe I should watch *Sesame Street*.
Malini: Definitely. Try it.
Kedar: I will. I have nothing to lose.
Malini: And your English will improve.
Kedar: I hope so.

COMPREHENSION

Answer these questions about the dialog. Use your own ideas to answer the question with an asterisk.

1. What is Kedar's favorite TV program?
2. What is Malini's favorite TV program?
3. Who is *Sesame Street* for?
4. What does Malini want Kedar to do?
5. What does he have to lose by watching *Sesame Street*?
*6. Do you think Kedar will like *Sesame Street*? Explain your answer.

SHARING INFORMATION

Discuss these questions in pairs, in small groups, or with the whole class.

1. What is your favorite TV program?
2. How much does it help you to learn English?

SENTENCE COMPLETION

Complete the sentences with these words.

should	losing	hope	definitely

1. I am _____ going to Rosa's party. She's my best friend.
3. The new restaurant is _____ money. It's going to close.
2. Charley is always tired. He _____ get more sleep.
4. I _____ my daughter goes to college.

trying	improving	news	kids

5. When I'm driving, I like to listen to the _____.
6. Allison is studying more, and her grades are _____.
7. It's hot and the _____ want to go for ice cream.
8. Adam is _____ to sell his car for $600.

MAKING COMPLETE SENTENCES

Draw lines from column A to column B to make complete sentences.

A	B
1. I always watch	older than I am.
2. The band practices a lot,	get more exercise.
3. Tony is definitely	and it's improving.
4. You should	is losing air.
5. The balloon	the 11 o'clock news.

Make complete sentences by joining the words from columns A and B.

Example

1. *I always watch the 11 o'clock news.* _____
2. _____
3. _____
4. _____
5. _____

A High School Principal

1. **until**   *I'll be back in two minutes. Stay here <u>until</u> I return.* **Until** means up to a certain time.

2. **respect**   *I love and <u>respect</u> my parents.* To **respect** is to have a high opinion of someone; to think highly of someone.

3. **strict**   *My grandparents let me do what I want, but my mom and dad are <u>strict</u>.* A **strict** person follows rules and makes others follow them.

4. **afraid (of)**   *Our boss gets angry a lot. That's why we're <u>afraid</u> of him.* **Afraid** means feeling fear. **Fear** is the feeling we get when we think that something bad may happen.

5. **fair**   *Our company gives everyone the same pay for the same work. That's <u>fair</u>.* To be **fair** is to treat everyone in a group in the same way. For example, a mother who treats all her children in the same way is fair.

6. **praise**   *The coach <u>praises</u> the team when it wins.* To **praise** is to say good things about someone or something.

7. **agree**   *Pete is a good friend, but there are many things we don't <u>agree</u> on.* To **agree** is to have the same opinion as another person.

124

PREVIEW QUESTIONS

Discuss these questions before listening to and reading the story.

1. Does a high school principal have a difficult job? Explain your answer.
2. Why should a principal listen to what the teachers have to say?

David Jackson is the principal of Kennedy High School. This is his third year as principal. There are 2,000 students in the high school. Mr. Jackson has a difficult job, but he loves his work.

Mr. Jackson works 12 hours a day. He gets up at five o'clock and is in school by six. He works until six at night. He has a sandwich and a cup of coffee for lunch. When he's very busy, he has a cup of coffee for lunch.

The teachers and parents like Mr. Jackson a lot. He always has time to listen to them. He respects them and their ideas, and they respect him.

Mr. Jackson is strict with the students, but they aren't afraid of him. They know that he's fair, and he often praises the students. Everyone agrees that Mr. Jackson is a good principal.

COMPREHENSION

Answer these questions about the story. Use your own ideas to answer the question with an asterisk.

Paragraph 1

1. What is David Jackson's job?
2. How many students are there in Kennedy High School?
3. How does Mr. Jackson feel about his job?

Paragraph 2

4. What time does Mr. Jackson get up?
5. What time does he get to school? What time does he finish work?
6. What does he have for lunch?

Paragraph 3

7. How do the parents and teachers feel about Mr. Jackson?
8. What does he always have time for?
9. How does he feel about the teachers and parents and their ideas?

Paragraph 4

10. Does Mr. Jackson let the students do what they want?
11. What do the students know about him?
12. What does everyone agree on?
*13. Do you also agree that Mr. Jackson is a good principal? Explain your answer.

SHARING INFORMATION

Discuss these questions in pairs, in small groups, or with the whole class.

1. Is it necessary for a high school principal to be strict with students? Explain your answer.
2. Do you think it's good for high school students to be afraid of their principal? Explain your answer.
3. How important is it for a principal to be fair with students?
4. Why is it important for teachers and principals to praise students?

SENTENCE COMPLETION

Complete the sentences with these words.

afraid	get up	fair	there are

1. I don't like to _____ in the morning, especially in the winter.
2. _____ a lot of stores in the mall.
3. Some people are _____ of dogs.
4. My teachers are _____. They act in the same way with all the students.

until	difficult	praises	busy

5. The barber shop is always _____ on Saturday.
6. It's _____ to be a good parent.
7. The children play in the yard _____ they get tired.
8. Carol is a great nurse. Everyone _____ her.

strict	principal	agree	respect

9. My son thinks he's a good driver, but I don't _____. He drives too fast.
10. A new teacher needs to be _____.
11. I _____ firefighters. Their work is dangerous.
12. The most important person in a school is the _____.

The Jackson Family

WORD BANK

1. **starve**   *I didn't eat breakfast today. I'm <u>starving</u>.* To **starve** is to be very hungry.
2. **as soon as**   *We'll leave <u>as soon as</u> you're ready.* **As soon as** means immediately after.
3. **nursery school**   *Michelle takes her son to a <u>nursery school</u> on her way to work.* A **nursery school** is a school for very young children.
4. **share**   *Our house is small. My two daughters have to <u>share</u> a room.* To **share** is to have or use something with another person.
5. **enough**   *We don't have <u>enough</u> money to buy a house.* **Enough** means as much as needed.
6. **promise**   *Steve <u>promises</u> to drive me to the airport.* To **promise** is to say that you definitely will or won't do something.

PREVIEW QUESTIONS

Discuss these questions before listening to and reading the story.

1. Do you think it's best for a mother with a young child (children) to stay at home to take care of her child (children), if possible? Explain your answer.
2. Why do many mothers go back to work soon after they have a child?

David and Linda Jackson are married and have two children, Eddie and Sara. Linda is a math teacher, but she's not teaching now. She stays home to take care of Eddie and Sara.

When David gets home from work, he's starving. So the family has dinner as soon as he gets home.

Eddie is eight and he's in the third grade. He likes school, and math is his favorite subject. He's also learning to play soccer and is taking piano lessons.

Sara is three and goes to nursery school three mornings a week. She is learning to play, work, and to share with other children. Her mom also reads to her a lot. Sara loves that.

Linda thinks David is a great principal. She also thinks he spends too much time at school and not enough time with Eddie and Sara. He knows Linda is right. So he promises to spend more time with his children on Saturday and Sunday.

COMPREHENSION

Answer these questions about the story. Use your own ideas to answer the question with an asterisk.

Paragraph 1

1. How many children do David and Linda have?
2. What subject does Linda teach?
3. Why isn't she teaching now?

Paragraph 2

4. How hungry is David when he gets home from work?
5. When does the family have dinner?

Paragraph 3

6. What grade is Eddie in?
7. What is his favorite subject?
8. What is he learning to play? What is he taking?

Paragraph 4

9. How often does Sara go to nursery school?
10. What is she learning at school?
11. What does Sara's mom do that Sara loves?
*12. Why is it good for parents to read to their children?

Paragraph 5

13. What does Linda think of David as a principal?
14. Why is she unhappy that David spends so much time at school?
15. What does he promise to do?

SHARING INFORMATION

Discuss these questions in pairs, in small groups, or with the whole class.

1. Is it natural for children to share? Or do parents and teachers have to teach them to share?
2. Why is it important for children to learn how to share?
3. How important is for fathers to spend a lot of time with their children? Why is it important?
4. Are fathers today more active in caring for their children than in the past?

SENTENCE COMPLETION

Complete the sentences with these words.

sharing	enough	stay	as soon as

1. I'm going for a walk _____ it stops raining.
2. Ken doesn't have _____ time to finish the test.
3. Nancy is _____ a box of candy with her friends.
4. Ashley wants to move to Florida, but her husband wants to _____ in New York

so	take care of	other	starving

5. Some students like our principal. _____ students think she's too strict.
6. Shawn has a toothache, _____ he's going to see a dentist.
7. I have to get something to eat. I'm _____.
8. My son is sick. I'm staying home from work to _____ him.

nursery school	too much	promises	spends

9. Ms. Johnson is a good teacher, but she gives _____ homework.
10. Joshua _____ a lot of time watching TV.
11. Lauren _____ to take her kids to the zoo to see the animals.
12. My son is making new friends at his _____.

MATCHING

Match the words in column A with their definitions or descriptions in column B. Print the letters on the blank lines.

Words from the Dialogs

Column A	Column B
_____ 1. around	A. maybe more but not less
_____ 2. improve	B. to like
_____ 3. at least	C. no doubt
_____ 4. have got to	D. close to; about
_____ 5. definitely	E. after that
_____ 6. accept	F. to be necessary
_____ 7. then	G. to get better
_____ 8. enjoy	H. to take an offer

Words from the Stories

Column A	Column B
_____ 1. praise	A. as much as needed
_____ 2. starve	B. to say you'll do something
_____ 3. agree	C. to think highly of someone
_____ 4. enough	D. to be very hungry
_____ 5. respect	E. up to a certain time
_____ 6. share	F. to say good things about someone
_____ 7. until	G. to use with another
_____ 8. promise	H. to have the same opinion

7

Food

Here are the people and characters you will meet in the dialogs and stories in this chapter.

Brian	Jessica	Allison
Danielle	Dick	Jennifer
Ray	Erica	Prince

No Breakfast This Morning

WORD BANK

1. **rush**   *The firefighters are <u>rushing</u> to the fire.* To **rush** is to move quickly.
2. **on time**   *I'm leaving for school now. I want to be <u>on time</u>.* **On time** is an expression that means not late.
3. **fire**   *Someday the boss is going to <u>fire</u> Tyler. He's very lazy.* To **fire** means to make someone leave a job.
4. **skip**   *Maria is going to <u>skip</u> basketball practice today, and the coach won't be happy.* To **skip** means to not do something.
5. **habit**   *I always brush my teeth before I go to bed. It's a <u>habit</u>.* A **habit** is something that you always do, often without thinking about it.

134

PREVIEW QUESTIONS

Discuss these questions before listening to and reading the dialog.

1. Are you always or almost always on time?
2. Why is it bad to be late for school or work?

Jessica is visiting her brother, Brian. He's rushing to get to work. He doesn't have time for breakfast.

Jessica: Why are you rushing?

Brian: To get to work on time.

Jessica: Will the boss be angry if you're late?

Brian: Definitely. He may fire me.

Jessica: Are you late much?

Brian: Yes, that's why he may fire me.

Jessica: And what are you having for breakfast?

Brian: Nothing. I rarely eat breakfast.

Jessica: Skipping breakfast is a bad habit.

Brian: I know, but I don't have time for it.

COMPREHENSION

Answer these questions about the dialog. Use your own ideas to answer the question with an asterisk.

1. Why is Brian rushing?
2. Will the boss be angry if Brian is late for work?
3. What may the boss do if he's late?
4. Is Brian late much?
5. What is he having for breakfast?
*6. Do you think Brian will be late for work this morning? Explain your answer.

SHARING INFORMATION

Discuss these questions in pairs, in small groups, or with the whole class.

1. What do you eat for breakfast?
2. Why is it bad to skip breakfast?

SENTENCE COMPLETION

Complete the sentences with these words.

rushing	definitely	fire	habit

1. Our boss is not doing a good job. The company is going to
   _____ him.
2. My computer is 10 years old. I _____ need a
   new one.
3. Smoking is a very bad _____.
4. George is _____ to the bank. It closes in five minutes.

get to	on time	skip	rarely

5. The train I take to work is always _____.
6. Andrea _____ eats ice cream or cake. She wants
   to lose weight.
7. What time did you _____ the party?
8. My friend and I like to walk in the park, but sometimes we
   _____ a day.

MAKING COMPLETE SENTENCES

Draw lines from column A to column B to make complete sentences.

A	B
1. The city is going to	to the accident.
2. Washing your hands before you eat	so I'm skipping some pages.
3. The police are rushing	is a good habit.
4. I want to read this book fast,	starts on time.
5. I hope the meeting	fire some of its workers.

Make complete sentences by joining the words from columns A and B.

Example

1. *The city is going to fire some of its workers.* _____
2. _____
3. _____
4. _____
5. _____

Lunch

WORD BANK

1. **so**   *Marissa is a secretary and <u>so</u> is her sister.* **So** means also; too.
2. **diner**   *This <u>diner</u> has great food. I think you'll like it.* A **diner** is a restaurant with a large menu and low prices.
3. **few**   *Ron is flying to Atlanta for a <u>few</u> days. He'll be back soon.* **Few** means a small number of.
4. **delicious**   *We love these cookies. They're <u>delicious</u>.* Food that tastes good is **delicious**.
5. **bowl**   *I'm having orange juice and a <u>bowl</u> of cereal for breakfast.* A **bowl** is a round dish in which we serve soup, cereal, salad, or fruit.

PREVIEW QUESTIONS

Discuss these questions before listening to and reading the dialog.

1. How often do you eat at a diner?
2. Do you think diners are good places to eat? Explain your answer.

It's Saturday and Brian and his sister, Jessica, are going to visit a friend. On the way, they stop to eat at a diner.

Jessica: I'm getting hungry.

Brian: So am I.

Jessica: Where can we stop?

Brian: There's a diner in a few miles.

Jessica: How's the food?

Brian: It's delicious.

Jessica: Let's stop there.

Brian: What are you getting?

Jessica: Salad and a bowl of soup.

Brian: I'm getting a turkey sandwich and ice cream.

COMPREHENSION

If the sentence is true, write T. *If it's false, write* F.

_____ 1. Jessica and Brian are getting hungry.
_____ 2. They stop at an expensive restaurant.
_____ 3. The food in the diner tastes good.
_____ 4. Jessica is getting soup and a salad.
_____ 5. Brian is getting a ham sandwich.

SHARING INFORMATION

Discuss these questions in pairs, in small groups, or with the whole class.

1. Name some foods that you think are delicious.
2. What is your favorite soup? What is your favorite ice cream?

SENTENCE COMPLETION

Complete the sentences with these words.

few	bowl	how's	so

1. Pat likes to play computer games and _____ do I.
2. There is a _____ of salad on the table.
3. The show will start in a _____ minutes.
4. _____ your new job?

delicious	let's	getting	diner

5. It's late. _____ go home.
6. Mmm! This cheeseburger is _____.
7. Is there a _____ near here? We want to get something to eat.
8. You'll need a coat. It's _____ cold.

MAKING COMPLETE SENTENCES

Draw lines from column A to column B to make complete sentences.

A	**B**
1. There are apples and oranges	at our favorite diner.
2. A few people	and so is her brother.
3. We are going to eat	are waiting for the bus.
4. These French fries	in the fruit bowl.
5. Cindy is rich,	are delicious.

Make complete sentences by joining the words from columns A and B.

Example

1. *There are apples and oranges in the fruit bowl.* _____
2. _____
3. _____
4. _____
5. _____

The Cake Looks Great

WORD BANK

1. **bake**   *Rebecca is <u>baking</u> a cake for her daughter's birthday.* To **bake** is to cook in an oven with dry heat.

2. **fry**   *I am going to <u>fry</u> some fish for dinner.* To **fry** is to cook in hot oil.

3. **prefer**   *Do you want to watch TV or do you <u>prefer</u> to go to the movies?* To **prefer** is to like one thing more than another.

4. **else**   *You have a good job and a nice family. What <u>else</u> do you want?* **Else** means more.

5. **how about**   *<u>How about</u> a cup of coffee?* **How about** is an expression. It means "*Do you want . . . ?*"

6. **dessert**   *We're having vanilla ice cream for <u>dessert</u>.* **Dessert** is food you eat at the end of dinner; for example, cake, pie, or ice cream.

PREVIEW QUESTIONS

Discuss these questions before listening to and reading the dialog.

1. Do you like chicken? Do you eat a lot of chicken?
2. Do you think it's better to bake chicken or to fry it? Explain your answer.

Brian and Allison are married, and both of them cook. Allison is cooking tonight. She is baking chicken. They're having cake for dessert.

Brian:	What are we having for dinner?
Allison:	Chicken.
Brian:	Are you going to bake or fry the chicken?
Allison:	Bake it.
Brian:	Good. What else are we having?
Allison:	Rice or spaghetti.
Brian:	I prefer spaghetti.
Allison:	OK. How about some cake for dessert?
Brian:	Sure. The cake looks great; I love cake.
Allison:	And so do I.

COMPREHENSION

Answer these questions about the dialog. Use your own ideas to answer the question with an asterisk.

1. What are Brian and Allison having for dinner?
2. How is Allison going to cook it?
3. What else are they having?
4. What are they having for dessert?
5. Do both Brian and Allison like cake a lot?
*6. Do you like cake a lot? What is your favorite dessert?

SHARING INFORMATION

Discuss these questions in pairs, in small groups, or with the whole class.

1. Do you like spaghetti? Do you eat it often?
2. Do you like rice? Do you eat it often? Do you prefer spaghetti or rice? Why?

SENTENCE COMPLETION

Complete the sentences with these words.

prefer	dessert	baking	so

1. Jason is _____ ham for dinner.
2. We're having fruit for _____. It's very healthy.
3. Victoria is a doctor and _____ is her husband.
4. Donald likes to take the train to Washington, D.C.
   I _____ to fly.

else	frying	great	how about

5. Brianna is _____ an egg for breakfast.
6. _____ a cold soda?
7. I know that you and Beth are going to the party. Who
   _____ is going?
8. It's _____ that Brett gets A's in all his subjects.

DIALOG REVIEW

Complete the paragraphs with these words.

A Delicious Dinner

fry	prefers	else	bake

Allison is cooking chicken for dinner. Brian asks if she is going to _____ or to _____ the chicken. Brian wants to know what _____ they're having. Allison says she's going to cook rice or spaghetti. Brian _____ spaghetti.

loves	dessert	so	great

Allison asks Brian if he wants some cake for _____. He says sure. He thinks the cake looks _____. He _____ cake and _____ does Allison.

ShopRite®

WORD BANK

1. **hate**   *Mark hates to work. He's lazy.* To **hate** is not to like something or somebody; to dislike. To **love** is the opposite of to hate.
2. **boring**   *The students don't like Mr. Green's class. It's boring.* **Boring** means not interesting.
3. **coupon**   *Mary cuts coupons from newspapers and magazines to use when she goes shopping.* A **coupon** is a piece of paper you can use to pay less to buy something.
4. **price**   *The price of this dress is too high. I'm not going to buy it.* **Price** is the money you have to pay to buy something.
5. **over**   *It takes me over an hour to get to work.* **Over** means more than.
6. **cheap**   *This is a good sweater, and it's cheap. I'm going to buy it.* **Cheap** means costing very little.

PREVIEW QUESTIONS

Discuss these questions before listening to and reading the dialog.

1. Who shops for food in your family?
2. What supermarket does that person go to?

Allison is talking to her friend Danielle about food shopping. They both go to ShopRite because it has good prices.

Allison: Do you like to shop for food?

Danielle: No. I hate it.

Allison: I do, too. It's boring.

Danielle: What supermarket do you go to?

Allison: ShopRite. It has good prices.

Danielle: I go there, too

Allison: Do you use coupons?

Danielle: Of course. It's an easy way to save money.

Allison: I spend over $100 a week at ShopRite.

Danielle: I spend about $200. Food isn't cheap.

COMPREHENSION

Answer these questions about the dialog. Use your own ideas to answer the question with an asterisk.

1. How does Danielle feel about shopping for food?
2. Why doesn't Allison like to shop for food?
3. What supermarket do Allison and Danielle go to?
4. Why does Danielle use coupons?
5. How much does Allison spend a week at ShopRite? And Danielle?
*6. Does anyone in your family use coupons at the supermarket?

SHARING INFORMATION

Discuss these questions in pairs, in small groups, or with the whole class.

1. About how much does your family spend a week at the supermarket?
2. Do you think it's boring to shop for food? Explain your answer.

SENTENCE COMPLETION

Complete the sentences with these words.

coupons	cheap	of course	hates

1. _____ it's expensive to travel.
2. I like to shop in stores that give _____.
3. Jonathan _____ to clean his room.
4. Tomatoes are _____ in the summer.

spends	boring	prices	over

5. The food at this restaurant is good, but the _____ are high.
6. I'm not going to read this book. It's _____.
7. My son is _____ six feet tall.
8. Diana _____ about two hours a night doing her homework.

MAKING COMPLETE SENTENCES

Draw lines from column A to column B to make complete sentences.

A	B
1. There are a lot of coupons	but she still drives.
2. I didn't like the show;	it's only $25.
3. My grandmother is over 80,	in today's newspaper.
4. I hate to	it was boring.
5. This watch is cheap;	study for tests.

Make complete sentences by joining the words from columns A and B.

Example

1. *There are a lot of coupons in today's newspaper.* _____
2. _____
3. _____
4. _____
5. _____

A Manager and a Police Officer

WORD BANK

1. **tough**   *Our math test was <u>tough</u>. I didn't do well on it.* **Tough** means difficult; hard.
2. **major**   *There is always a lot of traffic on Route 80. It's a <u>major</u> highway.* **Major** means very important; very large.
3. **hire**   *The factory is very busy. It's <u>hiring</u> more workers.* To **hire** is to give someone a job.
4. **play cards**   *I like to <u>play cards</u> with my friends.* To **play cards** is to play a game with a pack of cards, usually 52.
5. **neighbor**   *Bob lives across the street from me. We're <u>neighbors</u>.* A **neighbor** is a person who lives near you.
6. **worry**   *Erin <u>worries</u> when her daughter is out late at night.* To **worry** is to be afraid that something bad may happen.
7. **brave**   *Soldiers need to be <u>brave</u>.* **Brave** means willing to do what is very dangerous.
8. **protect**   *It's the job of parents to <u>protect</u> their children.* To **protect** is to keep bad things from happening to someone or something.

PREVIEW QUESTIONS

Discuss these questions before listening to and reading the story.

1. Does the manager of a large store have a hard job? Explain your answer.
2. Do you think that most managers work long hours? Do they get good pay?

Dick is the manager of the ShopRite where Allison and Danielle shop. It's a tough job. The store is big, and he has to take care of all of its major problems. He has to hire and sometimes fire workers. He works long hours, but the pay is good.

When Dick comes home, he watches TV or reads. He loves to read books about the history of the United States.

Dick and his wife, Jennifer, like to play cards. Every Friday night they play with some neighbors who come to their house. They never play for money. They play for fun.

Jennifer is a police officer. It's a dangerous job, and Dick worries about her. She's brave and likes her work. She says it gives her a chance to help and protect people.

COMPREHENSION

Answer these questions about the story. Use your own ideas to answer the question with an asterisk.

Paragraph 1

1. What is Dick's job?
2. Is the store large?
3. What does Dick have to take care of?

Paragraph 2

4. What does Dick do when he comes home from work?
5. What does he like to read?

Paragraph 3

6. What do Dick and Jennifer like to do?
7. Who do they play with?
8. What do they play for?

Paragraph 4

9. What is Jennifer's job?
10. Why does Dick worry about her?
11. What chance does Jennifer's job give her?
*12. Police officers protect people. What else do they protect?

SHARING INFORMATION

Discuss these questions in pairs, in small groups, or with the whole class.

1. How do you relax when you come home from work or school?
2. Do you like to play cards? Do you play much?
3. Who do you play with?
4. Do you think it's OK for adults to play cards for money? Explain your answer.

SENTENCE COMPLETION

Complete the sentences with these words.

brave	fun	protects	neighbor

1. The children had _____ at the park.
2. Jack is a good _____. He helps us when he can.
3. You have to be _____ to be a firefighter.
4. We have a big dog. He _____ us and our home.

dangerous	hiring	worry	major

5. Our company is losing money. It has to make some _____ changes.
6. I don't smoke. It's too _____.
7. My father is sick. I _____ about him.
8. The restaurant is _____ another cook.

playing cards	fire	tough	take care of

9. It's _____ to work with teenagers.
10. Ben spends a lot of time _____ with his friends.
11. It very important to _____ your health.
12. Our basketball team rarely wins. They're going to _____ the coach.

Two Children and Prince

WORD BANK

1. **engineer**   *Alice is an <u>engineer</u>. She is working on the plans for the new highway.* An **engineer** is a person who plans machines, roads, and bridges.

2. **fan**   *Gino is a soccer <u>fan</u>. He goes to a lot of soccer games and watches them on TV.* A **fan** is a person who has a special interest in a sport.

3. **strong**   *Mike gets a lot of exercise. That's why he's so <u>strong</u>.* **Strong** means having a lot of physical power.

4. **freshman**   *Ann is graduating from high school in June. In September, she'll be a <u>freshman</u> in college.* A **freshman** is a student who is in the first year of high school or college.

5. **bark**   *Most people are afraid of our dog when they hear her <u>bark</u> and see how big she is.* To **bark** is to make the sound a dog makes.

6. **feed**   *The baby is hungry. I have to <u>feed</u> her.* To **feed** is to give food to a person or animal.

150

PREVIEW QUESTIONS

Discuss these questions before listening to and reading the story.

1. What do you know about engineers? Do they need a college education? Do they have to know math? Do they make good money?
2. Are you a sports fan? If you are, what sport or sports do you like?

Dick and Jennifer have two children, Ray and Erica. Ray is a junior in high school. He's 16 years old. He does well in math and wants to be an engineer.

Ray likes music and plays in the school band. He's also a big football fan, but he's not big or strong enough to play football. In the fall, he often watches football on TV.

Erica is a freshman in high school. She's 14. She's a very good volleyball player. She also loves computers and knows a lot about them. She's going to study computer science in college. After she graduates, she hopes to work with computers.

The family also has a dog. His name is Prince. Everyone likes him. He's very friendly and doesn't bark much. Jennifer usually feeds Prince. He loves her more than anyone.

COMPREHENSION

Answer these questions about the story. Use your own ideas to answer the question with an asterisk.

Paragraph 1

1. How many children do Dick and Jennifer have? What are their names?
2. How old is their son?
3. What does he want to be?

Paragraph 2

4. How do we know that Ray likes music?
5. In what sport does he have a special interest?
6. Why doesn't he play that sport?

Paragraph 3

7. How old is Erica?
8. What does she love and know a lot about?
9. What does she hope to do after she graduates from college?

Paragraph 4

10. Why does everyone like Prince?
11. Why does he love Jennifer more than anyone?
*12. Do you think it's better to have a dog that barks a lot or one that doesn't bark much? Explain your answer.

SHARING INFORMATION

Discuss these questions in pairs, in small groups, or with the whole class.

1. They say a dog is man's best friend. What does that mean? Do you think that's true?
2. Do you have a dog or other pet? If so, tell us about your dog or other pet.
3. Do you like to use computers? Do you use them much?
4. Do you use e-mail? Do you use it much?

SENTENCE COMPLETION

Complete the sentences with these words.

strong	band	friendly	freshman

1. It's easy to talk to Alan. He's very _____.
2. I need a _____ person to help me move this piano.
3. Ed is going to begin high school in September. He'll be a _____.
4. I like the way the _____ plays. It's very good.

barks	graduate	enough	engineer

5. Juana will be the first one in her family to _____ from college.
6. You have to study a lot to become an _____.
7. Our dog _____ too much, but it won't be easy to change him.
8. Do we have _____ food for the party?

feed	usually	fans	junior

9. There are many baseball _____ in Japan.
10. I _____ eat lunch at one o'clock.
11. Kim is in her second year of college. Next year, she'll be a _____.
12. In the winter, I _____ the birds every day.

MATCHING

Match the words in Column A with their definitions or descriptions in Column B. Print the letters on the blank lines.

Words from the Dialogs

Column A	Column B
_____ **1.** bake	**A.** not late
_____ **2.** few	**B.** to move quickly
_____ **3.** dessert	**C.** a restaurant with low prices
_____ **4.** rush	**D.** a small number of
_____ **5.** over	**E.** not interesting
_____ **6.** diner	**F.** cake, pie, ice cream
_____ **7.** boring	**G.** to cook in an oven
_____ **8.** on time	**H.** more than

Words from the Stories

Column A	Column B
_____ **1.** hire	**A.** difficult
_____ **2.** engineer	**B.** a person who lives near you
_____ **3.** tough	**C.** to make the sound a dog makes
_____ **4.** feed	**D.** a person who loves a sport
_____ **5.** neighbor	**E.** to give someone a job
_____ **6.** fan	**F.** very important
_____ **7.** major	**G.** to give someone food
_____ **8.** bark	**H.** a person who plans roads

8 Weather and Newcomers

Here are the people you will meet in the dialogs and stories in this chapter.

Pierre

Nicole

Matt

Lin Wu

Chen Wu

Karen Wu

Eric Wu

My Favorite Season

🎧 WORD BANK

1. **season**   *I think fall is the nicest <u>season</u> of the year*. There are four **seasons**; spring, summer, fall, and winter.
2. **bother**   *I'm trying to study. That music is <u>bothering</u> me*. To **bother** is to cause a problem for someone; to make someone unhappy.
3. **be used to**   *Betty works in a factory. She <u>is used to</u> hard work*. To **be used to** is to be familiar with something; to have experience with something.
4. **shovel**   *Jesse is <u>shoveling</u> snow in front of his house*. To **shovel** is to move snow or earth with a shovel.

PREVIEW QUESTIONS

Discuss these questions before reading and listening to the dialog.

1. What is your favorite season? Why?
2. Is there a season you don't like? If so, which one? Why?

Nicole and Pierre are at a party. He's from Haiti. He loves to go to the beach in the summer, but he hates winter.

Nicole:	What's your favorite season?
Pierre:	Summer. I like to go to the beach.
Nicole:	Does hot weather ever bother you?
Pierre:	Never. I love it.
Nicole:	Is there a season you don't like?
Pierre:	Winter. I hate cold weather.
Nicole:	Where are you from?
Pierre:	Haiti. I'm not used to the cold.
Nicole:	Do you like snow?
Pierre:	It's pretty, but I don't like to shovel it.

COMPREHENSION

Answer these questions about the dialog. Use your own ideas to answer the question with an asterisk.

1. What is Pierre's favorite season?
2. What does he like to do in the summer?
3. What does he hate?
4. Why isn't he used to cold weather?
5. What doesn't he like to do?
*6. Do you think it ever snows in Haiti? Explain your answer.

SHARING INFORMATION

Discuss these questions in pairs, in small groups, or with the whole class.

1. Does hot weather ever bother you? Does it bother you a lot?
2. Do you like snow? Explain your answer?

SENTENCE COMPLETION

Complete the sentences with these words.

season	hates	shovels	favorite

1. My grandfather is 65, but he still _____ snow.
2. Kyle _____ to go to the dentist.
3. Orange juice is my _____ drink.
4. Summer is the _____ when most people go on vacation.

bothers	ever	used to	beach

5. Do you _____ take the children to the park?
6. In July and August, I like to go to the _____ to swim.
7. It _____ our principal when students are late for school.
8. Nurses are _____ caring for the sick.

MAKING COMPLETE SENTENCES

Draw lines from column A to column B to make complete sentences.

A	B
1. What season	getting what he wants.
2. Angela loves to eat	to shovel.
3. We have a lot of snow	begins in September?
4. The president is used to	doesn't answer my e-mail.
5. It bothers me when my brother	but hates to cook.

Make complete sentences by joining the words from columns A and B.

Example

1. *What season begins in September?*
2. _____
3. _____
4. _____
5. _____

What Are You Wearing?

🎧 **WORD BANK**

1. **wear**   *Jerry is <u>wearing</u> a white shirt.* To **wear** is to have on your body, especially clothes.
2. **suit**   *Doug always wears a <u>suit</u> to work.* A **suit** is a jacket and pants made of the same material.
3. **put on**   *Amanda is <u>putting on</u> her blue sweater.* To **put on** is to put clothes on your body.
4. **freezing**   *It's <u>freezing</u> out. You'll need your winter coat.* **Freezing** means very cold.
5. **gloves**   *I always wear <u>gloves</u> when I go out in cold weather.* **Gloves** are what we wear on our hands.
6. **closet**   *There are many dresses in Debra's <u>closet</u>.* A **closet** is a small area where we keep clothes.

PREVIEW QUESTIONS

Discuss these questions before reading and listening to the dialog.

1. When do we usually wear a suit?
2. What do you wear when it's cold out?

Matt and Nicole are married. They're going to a wedding. He's wearing a black suit, and she's wearing a red dress.

Nicole:	What are you wearing to the wedding?
Matt:	My new black suit.
Nicole:	I'm wearing a red dress.
Matt:	Are you almost ready?
Nicole:	Yes, I'm putting on my shoes.
Matt:	How cold is it out?
Nicole:	Very. It's freezing.
Matt:	Did you see my gloves?
Nicole:	They're in the closet.
Matt:	Good. Let's go. It's getting late.

COMPREHENSION

If the sentence is true, write T. *If it's false, write* F.

_____ 1. Matt is wearing a suit to the wedding.
_____ 2. Nicole is wearing a skirt.
_____ 3. It's very cold out.
_____ 4. Nicole knows where Matt's gloves are.
_____ 5. He wants to leave in 20 minutes.

SHARING INFORMATION

Discuss these questions in pairs, in small groups, or with the whole class.

1. What do you usually wear to school or to work?
2. What do you like to wear when it's hot out?

SENTENCE COMPLETION

Complete the sentences with these words.

wedding	putting on	suit	freezing

1. Omar is _____ his raincoat.
2. Close the windows. This room is _____.
3. Jeff and Sarah are planning their _____.
   They're getting married in a year.
4. I need to buy a new _____.

gloves	ready	closet	wear

5. The _____ in our bedroom is small.
6. Melissa is _____ to go to work.
7. Many students _____ jeans to school.
8. I like these _____. They keep my hands warm.

MAKING COMPLETE SENTENCES

Draw lines from column A to column B to make complete sentences.

A	B
1. Joe is putting on sneakers	too small for me.
2. This suit is	you'll need a hat.
3. Our new house	to play basketball.
4. It's freezing;	I like to wear shorts.
5. In the summer,	has four large closets.

Make complete sentences by joining the words from columns A and B.

Example

1. *Joe is putting on sneakers to play basketball.*
2. _____
3. _____
4. _____
5. _____

Sunny and Warmer

WORD BANK

1. **hike**   *On Saturday, Nick and I are going for a five-mile <u>hike</u>.* A **hike** is a long walk in the country.
2. **plenty (of)**   *There was <u>plenty</u> of food at the picnic.* **Plenty** means a lot (of).
3. **cloudy**   *We won't get any sun today. It's going to be <u>cloudy</u>.* Drops of water form **clouds** in the sky. **Cloudy** means with many clouds.
4. **shower**   *It's not raining now, but we're going to get some <u>showers</u> this afternoon.* A **shower** is a short period of rain.
5. **sunny**   *In the summer, we get many <u>sunny</u> days.* **Sunny** means with a lot of sun.
6. **terrific**   *We learn a lot in Mrs. Brown's class. She's a <u>terrific</u> teacher.* **Terrific** means great.

PREVIEW QUESTIONS

Discuss these questions before reading and listening to the dialog.

1. Do you like to go for hikes? How often do you go for one?
2. Who do you go with? What do you wear?

Today's weather report is cloudy with showers, but tomorrow is going to be sunny. Matt and Nicole are going for a hike tomorrow.

Nicole:	Where are we going for our hike?
Matt:	To the state park.
Nicole:	That's a great place for a hike.
Matt:	Are we bringing lunch?
Nicole:	Yes, we'll have plenty to eat.
Matt:	What's today's weather report?
Nicole:	Cloudy with a few showers.
Matt:	And tomorrow's?
Nicole:	Sunny and warmer.
Matt:	That's terrific.

COMPREHENSION

Answer these questions about the dialog. Use your own ideas to answer the question with an asterisk.

1. Where are Matt and Nicole going for their hike?
2. Does Nicole think that's a good place for a hike?
3. Are they going to buy their lunch?
4. What's today's weather report?
5. What's tomorrow's report?
*6. Why is a state park a good place for a hike?

SHARING INFORMATION

Discuss these questions in pairs, in small groups, or with the whole class.

1. Why is going for a hike good for you?
2. What do you think is the best season for a hike? Explain your answer.

SENTENCE COMPLETION

Complete the sentences with these words.

terrific	plenty	showers	cloudy

1. In April, we usually get a lot of _____.
2. Muhammad Ali was a _____ boxer.
3. It's _____ and cold this morning, and it's going to snow this afternoon.
4. Kelly has _____ of money. She can buy any car she wants.

sunny	great	hike	few

5. San Francisco is a _____ city to visit.
6. The weather report says it's going to be _____ today.
7. Scott has a cold, but he'll be fine in a _____ days.
8. After our _____, we were tired and hungry.

DIALOG REVIEW

Complete the paragraphs with these words.

A Long Walk in the State Park

bringing	hike	plenty	great

Matt and Nicole are going for a _____ in the state park. It's a _____ place for a long walk. Matt and Nicole are their lunch. They'll have _____ to eat.

sunny	showers	terrific	cloudy

Nicole says that it's going to be _____ today with _____. Tomorrow will be _____ and warmer. Matt says that's _____.

A Hurricane

1. **what's the matter?** *"Why are you crying? <u>What's the matter?</u>"* **What's the matter?** is an expression. It means "What's the problem?"
2. **hurricane** *They get a lot of <u>hurricanes</u> in the Caribbean and Florida.* A **hurricane** is a tropical storm with very strong winds and heavy rain.
3. **warning** *On every pack of cigarettes, there is a <u>warning</u> that smoking cigarettes is dangerous to your health.* A **warning** is a statement that something is dangerous, that something bad may happen.
4. **wind** *The flag in the park isn't moving. There's very little <u>wind</u> today.* **Wind** is air that is moving.
5. **immediately** *"Come here <u>immediately</u>. I have to show you something."* **Immediately** means now; without delay.
6. **pack** *Sandra is <u>packing</u> her lunch to take to work.* To **pack** is to put something in a bag or box to take somewhere.
7. **hurry** *Larry is <u>hurrying</u> to get to school on time.* To **hurry** is to move quickly.

PREVIEW QUESTIONS

Discuss these questions before reading and listening to the dialog.

1. Name some countries, in addition to the United States, that get hurricanes.
2. Does your home country get hurricanes? Does it get many?

Matt and Nicole live in New Jersey, near the ocean. Nicole tells Matt there is a hurricane warning.

Nicole:	Matt! Matt!
Matt:	What's the matter, Nicole?
Nicole:	We have a hurricane warning!
Matt:	Oh, no!
Nicole:	We're going to get winds of 120 miles an hour.
Matt:	That's dangerous.
Nicole:	We should leave immediately.
Matt:	I agree.
Nicole:	Let's start packing the car!
Matt:	OK. We have to hurry.

COMPREHENSION

Answer these questions about the dialog. Use your own ideas to answer the question with an asterisk.

1. What does Nicole tell Matt?
2. How fast are the winds going to be?
3. When does Nicole want to leave?
4. What does she say they should start to do?
5. What does Matt say to her about packing the car?
*6. Do you think Nicole and Matt are smart to leave immediately? Explain your answer.

SHARING INFORMATION

Discuss these questions in pairs, in small groups, or with the whole class.

1. What do you think Nicole and Matt are going to pack?
2. Will they have to drive slowly? Why?

SENTENCE COMPLETION

Complete the sentences with these words.

packing	hurricane	immediately	hurrying

1. Call 911 and you'll get help _____.
2. I'm afraid that we're going to get a _____.
3. Courtney is _____ to get to the post office before it closes.
4. Jared is _____ the books he needs for school.

wind	agree	what's the matter	warning

5. You're very angry. _____?
6. It's cold out and the _____ makes it feel colder.
7. Did you read the _____? It says that the lake is very deep.
8. I think I should get more money, but my boss doesn't _____.

MAKING COMPLETE SENTENCES

Draw lines from column A to column B to make complete sentences.

A	B
1. The hurricane season	go to Mexico.
2. Go to the hospital	begins in June.
3. We're packing to	on the medicine bottle.
4. Julia likes to work slowly;	immediately.
5. There is a warning	she hates to hurry.

Make complete sentences by joining the words from columns A and B.

Example

1. *The hurricane season begins in June.*_____
2. _____
3. _____
4. _____
5. _____

From China to the United States

WORD BANK

1. **Chinatown**   *When we go to New York City, we like to eat in <u>Chinatown</u>.* **Chinatown** is an area of a city where a large number of Chinese live.

2. **own**   *Ryan and Michelle <u>own</u> a house and two cars.* To **own** is to have something; to possess something.

3. **grocery store**   *I'm going to the <u>grocery store</u> to get milk and bread.* A **grocery store** sells food and small things used in a home.

4. **miss**   *My wife is in Chicago for a few days. I <u>miss</u> her.* To **miss** is to feel sad because someone you like is not with you.

5. **opportunity**   *Jamal has the <u>opportunity</u> to get a better job.* An **opportunity** is the chance to do something.

6. **freedom**   *Today, the people in many countries enjoy <u>freedom</u>.* **Freedom** is the ability to do or say what you wish.

168

PREVIEW QUESTIONS

Discuss these questions before listening to and reading the story.

1. Do you still miss your home country? What do you miss?
2. Who do you miss?

Lin and Chen Wu are married and live in Chinatown in Manhattan. They own a Chinese grocery store on Canal Street, a busy street in Chinatown. Their store is open seven days a week, from seven in the morning to eight at night.

Lin and Chen still miss China, but they like living in the United States. They like the opportunities this country offers them and their children. They enjoy the freedom they have here.

There is one thing that Lin and Chen don't like about New York—the cold weather and snow. They're from a town in China where it's very hot in the summer and warm in the winter. It never snows there.

Lin and Chen speak Chinese in their store and at home. They understand English, but can't speak it well. They want to go to school to learn more English, but they're too busy working in their store.

COMPREHENSION

Answer these questions about the story. Use your own ideas to answer the question with an asterisk.

Paragraph 1

1. Where do Lin and Chen Wu live?
2. What do they own?
3. When is their store open?

Paragraph 2

4. What do Lin and Chen still miss?
5. What does the United States offer them and their children?
6. What do they enjoy in the United States?

Paragraph 3

7. What is the one thing Lin and Chen don't like about New York?
8. Describe the summer weather in the town they're from.
9. Describe the weather there in the winter.
10. How often does it snow there?

Paragraph 4

11. What language do Lin and Chen speak at home?
12. Is it easier for them to understand English or to speak it?
13. Why don't they go to school to learn more English?
*14. Is it easier for you to understand English or to speak it? Explain your answer.

SHARING INFORMATION

Discuss these questions in pairs, in small groups, or with the whole class.

1. Do you think it's easy or hard to own and work in a grocery store? Explain your answer.
2. Is the United States still a land of opportunity for most immigrants? Explain your answer.
3. Do you think the United States is a land of opportunity for you? Explain your answer.
4. Do you think women in the United States have more freedom than women in your home country? Explain your answer.

SENTENCE COMPLETION

Complete the sentences with these words.

miss	busy	freedom	there

1. Sometimes people have to fight for their _____.
2. I can't help you now. I'm very _____.
3. We're going to visit Boston. There are a lot of things to see _____.
4. Our daughter is staying with her grandmother for the weekend. We _____ her.

warm	offer	grocery store	still

5. I usually go to the supermarket, but sometimes I go to the _____ near my house.
6. The room is _____. You won't need a sweater.
7. Is Vanessa _____ reading the newspaper?
8. I'm going to _____ to help Brandon with his homework.

enjoy	opportunity	own	well

9. Chris has the _____ to play soccer on a good team.
10. Tiffany is taking singing lessons. She sings _____.
11. Jacob and Caroline have a nice house. They also _____ a small boat.
12. We _____ watching TV after dinner.

Eager to Learn

JUDGE WU

WORD BANK

1. **sophomore** *Jackie is a sophomore. Next September, she'll be a junior.* A **sophomore** is a student in the second year of high school or college.

2. **hard** *It's snowing hard. We won't have school today.* **Hard** means a lot; very much. (**Hard** also means difficult. See page 11.)

3. **obey** *It's important for children to obey their parents.* To **obey** is to do what someone tells you to do.

4. **pharmacy** *Doctor Robinson teaches pharmacy in college.* **Pharmacy** is the study of preparing and selling medicines. (A **pharmacy** is also a store where you buy medicines.)

5. **already** *It's raining already. Take an umbrella.* **Already** means before now or now.

6. **eager** *Pedro is eager to go to college.* **Eager** means having a strong desire to do something.

PREVIEW QUESTIONS

Discuss these questions before listening to and reading the story.

1. Asian students respect their teachers a lot. Does this help them to learn? How?
2. How important is it that students obey their teachers? Explain your answer.

Lin and Chen Wu have two children, Karen and Eric. Karen is 12 and is in the seventh grade. Eric is 15 and is a sophomore at Seward Park High School in Chinatown.

Karen and Eric are very good students. They respect their teachers a lot. They always do their homework and study hard for their tests. They obey their teachers. They're eager to learn.

Like their parents, Karen and Eric love hot weather. In the summer, they enjoy swimming and playing tennis. Karen is an excellent swimmer. Eric plays tennis for Seward Park High School.

Karen wants to go to college and study pharmacy. She's already interested in medicine and knows a lot about it. Science is her favorite subject. Eric wants to be a lawyer. His favorite subjects are history and English.

COMPREHENSION

Answer these questions about the story. Use your own ideas to answer the question with an asterisk.

Paragraph 1

1. How many children do Lin and Chen Wu have?
2. How old is Karen? What grade is she in?
3. How old is Eric? What year of high school is he in?

Paragraph 2

4. How do Karen and Eric feel about their teachers?
5. How do they prepare for their tests?
6. When a teacher tells them to do something, what do they do?

Paragraph 3

7. How are Karen and Eric like their parents?
8. What do they enjoy doing in the summer?
9. Who does Eric play tennis for?

Paragraph 4

10. What does Karen want to study in college?
11. What is her favorite subject?
12. What does Eric want to be?
13. What are his favorite subjects?
*14. English is one of Eric's favorite subjects. How will knowing English well make him a better lawyer?

SHARING INFORMATION

Discuss these questions in pairs, in small groups, or with the whole class.

1. Do you think students in your home country have more respect for teachers than students in the United States? Explain your answer.
2. It's important for students to respect their teachers. How important is it that students also respect other students? Explain your answer.
3. Karen wants to be a pharmacist. Do you think that is an interesting job? Do you think it pays well?
4. Why do pharmacists have to continue to read and to learn more all the time?

SENTENCE COMPLETION

Complete the sentences with these words.

obey	like	already	pharmacy

1. Aaron is home _____. He's early today.
2. When a police officer tells you to stop, you have to
_____.
3. It's not easy to study _____. There's so much to learn.
4. Janet looks _____ her sister.

excellent	respects	sophomore	eager

5. My daughter is _____ to learn to drive.
6. Christina is a very good person. Everyone _____ her.
7. My children go to an _____ school. They're learning a lot.
8. It's much easier to be a _____ than a freshman.

hard	medicine	lawyer	interested

9. This _____ is expensive, but the doctor wants me to take it.
10. Brett is a mechanic, and he works _____.
11. I'm not _____ in going to the movies tonight.
12. Before you talk to the police, you should see a
_____.

MATCHING

Match the words in column A with their definitions or descriptions in column B. Print the letters on the blank lines.

Words from the Dialogs

Column A	Column B
_____ 1. freezing	A. a long walk
_____ 2. hurry	B. to make someone unhappy
_____ 3. hike	C. where we keep clothes
_____ 4. terrific	D. to move quickly
_____ 5. closet	E. a lot
_____ 6. immediately	F. great
_____ 7. bother	G. very cold
_____ 8. plenty	H. now

Words from the Stories

Column A	Column B
_____ 1. pharmacy	A. having a strong desire to
_____ 2. own	B. a chance to do something
_____ 3. eager	C. a lot; very much
_____ 4. already	D. to do what someone tells you
_____ 5. opportunity	E. the study of medicines
_____ 6. obey	F. it sells food
_____ 7. grocery store	G. to have something
_____ 8. hard	H. before now; now

Word List

Alphabetical list of words defined in the **Word Banks**.

A

about *adv.* 90
accept *v.* 112
afraid (of) *adj.* 124
agree *v.* 124
alike *adj.* 102
already *adv.* 172
also *adv.* 14
angry *adj.* 102
another *pron.* 74
apartment *n.* 14
apply *v.* 112
around *prep.* 46
around *prep.* 115
as soon as *conj.* 128
at first *expression* 80
at least *expression* 112

B

bake *v.* 140
band *n.* 84
bank teller *n.* 80
barber *n.* 74
bark *v.* 150
be at home *expression* 58
be back *expression* 96
be used to *expression* 156
beach *n.* 80
become *v.* 71
bedroom *n.* 14
best *adj.* 40
better *adj.* 143
boring *adj.* 40
both *pron.* 102
bother *v.* 156
bowl *n.* 137
boyfriend *n.* 24
brave *adj.* 146
busy *adj.* 52

C

camera *n.* 80
can't *v.* 11
cashier *n.* 36
cell phone *n.* 8
chance *n.* 62
cheap *adj.* 143
child *n.* 14
Chinatown *n.* 168

clear *adj.* 68
closet *n.* 159
cloudy *adj.* 162
coach *n.* 40
concert *n.* 115
congratulations *n.* 33
cost *v.* 80
coupon *n.* 143
cousin *n.* 58
crazy about *expression* 106
custodian *n.* 62
customer *n.* 36
cut *v.* 74
cute *adj.* 33

D

dangerous *adj.* 99
definitely *adv.* 121
delicious *adj.* 137
dental hygienist *n.* 80
dessert *n.* 140
different *adj.* 58
diner *n.* 137
dinner *n.* 8
Dominican Republic, the *n.* 58
doubt *v.* 93
dream *n.* 40
drum *n.* 84

E

eager *adj.* 172
earring *n.* 30
else *adv.* 140
emergency room *n.* 71
engineer *n.* 150
enjoy *v.* 115
enough *adj.* 128
especially *adv.* 93
excellent *adj.* 49
exciting *adj.* 99
exercise *n.* 96
expensive *adj.* 84

F

factory *n.* 62
fair *adj.* 124
fan *n.* 150
far *adv.* 90
favorite *adj.* 18
feed *v.* 150

few *adj.* 137
field *n.* 58
fine *adj.* 33
fire *v.* 134
firefighter *n.* 74
football *n.* 99
forget *v.* 30
free time *expression* 74
freedom *n.* 168
freezing *adj.* 159
frequently *adv.* 84
fresh air *expression* 96
freshman *n.* 150
friend *n.* 5
fry *v.* 140
fun *n.* 93

G

get up *v.* 118
get *v.* 30
glad *adj.* 2
gloves (plural) *n.* 159
government *n.* 36
grade *n.* 18
grade *n.* 112
graduate *v.* 80
grandmother *n.* 33
grandson *n.* 52
great *adj.* 49
grocery store *n.* 168
guidance counselor *n.* 36

H

habit *n.* 134
Haiti *n.* 156
handsome *adj.* 84
happy *adj.* 2
hard *adj.* 11
hard *adv.* 172
hate *v.* 143
have go to *expression* 118
health *n.* 49
heavy *adj.* 102
hello *expression* 2
he's *contraction* 5
hi *expression* 2
hike *n.* 162
hire *v.* 146
homework *n.* 8